北京第二外国语学院资助出版教材

刘振聪◎主编　　贾彤　耿恺婕◎副主编

A COLLECTION OF EXERCISES IN LINGUISTICS

语言学习题汇编

北京·旅游教育出版社

前　言

普通语言学以人类所有语言为对象，研究语言的一般性质和共同规律。普通语言学的理论原则对具体语言的研究具有指导作用。普通语言学理论的学习，重点包括掌握语言研究的三个层面，即音系、句法和语义，同时了解语言与文化、社会及语境等因素的关系。

本书内容包括：普通语言学及其研究领域；语言学流派及其理论方法，包括描写语言学、功能语言学、结构主义语言学、转换生成语法等；语言结构系统，包括音系学、词汇学、形态学、句法学、语义学和语用学；语言学与相关学科的关系，包括心理语言学、神经语言学、认知语言学、语言与文化、文体学、语料库语言学、社会语言学和应用语言学等。

本书亮点如下：

- 直接脱胎于课堂讲稿及训练，通俗易懂；
- 内容全面，涵盖语言学主要相关研究领域；
- 练习丰富，与考研、考博及资格考试紧密结合；
- 重点突出，每章都配有思维导图，方便掌握。

那么，如何使用本书呢？编者认为，读者应该在打好基础的前提下使用本书，因为本书的主要目的在于提供检测手段和参考资源。读者最好通读一本或多本语言学专著，对其中的基本概念、理论和方法有了深入的了解，并且能够融会贯通，而后使用本书进行检验和测试，匡谬正误，拾遗补缺。

答题建议如下：答案必须全面、详细，而且有条理；适当引用相关理论作答，答案包括一些对具体研究和发现的讨论，在适当的情况下，还涉及反驳的论点，证明你对相关文献有全面的了解，并且具备清晰有条理地阐释和应用相关知识的能力；答案分析合乎逻辑，语言清晰、流畅、有效；使用正确的句法和基本语法规则，包括拼写、标点符号、大写、缩写和引用等。

为了阐明做题方法，下文以简答题和阐述题为例说明。请看以下三例：

(1) **Spatial Relation:** A relationship, based on spatio-geometric properties, that holds between a figure and a reference object. For instance, in an utterance such as: *The bike is beside the building,* a spatial relation of proximity and adjacency is designated by the preposition *beside* and what we know about the nature of bikes, buildings and how they are normally located with respect to one another.

(2) **Closed Class Forms:** A set of linguistic forms to which it is typically more difficult for a language to add new members. Closed class forms are normally taken to include the "grammatical" or "function" words of a language. In English these include articles, prepositions, pronouns, inflectional morphemes and so forth. In terms of the meaning contributed by the closed class elements they provide schematic meaning. They contribute to the interpretation of an utterance in important but often subtle ways, providing a kind of "scaffolding" which supports and structures the content meaning provided by open class forms.

(3) **Cognitive Linguistics:** A school of linguistics and cognitive science which emerged from the early 1980s onwards. Places central importance on the role of meaning, conceptual processes and embodied experience in the study of language and the mind and the way in which they intersect. Cognitive linguistics is an enterprise or an approach to the study of language and the mind rather than a single articulated theoretical framework. It is informed by two overarching principles or commitments: the generalization commitment and the cognitive commitment. The two best developed sub-branches of cognitive linguistics are cognitive semantics and cognitive approaches to grammar. While cognitive linguistics began to emerge in the 1980s as a broadly grounded intellectual movement, it traces its roots to work that was taking place in the 1970s, particularly in the United States, which was reacting to formal linguistics. Early pioneers in the 1970s who were instrumental in formulating this new approach include *Gilles Fauconnier, Charles Fillmore, George Lakoff, Ronald Langacker* and *Leonard Talmy*.

例（1）是定义性解释，外加实例；适用于简答题，不适用于阐述题。例（2）是阐释性解释，有适度的扩展和个人理解；适用于简答题，不适用于阐述题。例（3）主要是阐释，有大量的扩展，包括定义、历史、特性、构成、代表人物等；篇幅较长，适用于阐述题。

本书适用于对语言学感兴趣的读者、英语专业本科生、考研准备者、语言学专业研究生和博士生以及担任语言学课程的教师。

本书由刘振聪担任主编,负责全书的统稿工作;贾彤和耿恺婕共同担任副主编。具体编写分工如下:刘振聪负责第1章至第5章、第12章至第16章、每章前面的思维导图;贾彤负责第6章至第8章;耿恺婕负责第9章至第11章。

囿于编者水平有限,疏漏和不足之处在所难免,还请各位专家、学者不吝赐教,也恳请各位同行和读者提出宝贵的意见和建议,以便我们及时修改和不断完善。

刘振聪

2018年5月

于京东翰墨斋

Contents 目录

Chapter 1
Language and Linguistics / 语言和语言学 ⋯⋯⋯⋯⋯⋯⋯⋯⋯⋯⋯⋯ 1

Chapter 2
Phonetics and Phonology / 语音学和音素学 ⋯⋯⋯⋯⋯⋯⋯⋯⋯ 17

Chapter 3
Morphology / 形态学 ⋯⋯⋯⋯⋯⋯⋯⋯⋯⋯⋯⋯⋯⋯⋯⋯⋯⋯⋯ 29

Chapter 4
Semantics / 语义学 ⋯⋯⋯⋯⋯⋯⋯⋯⋯⋯⋯⋯⋯⋯⋯⋯⋯⋯⋯⋯ 39

Chapter 5
Syntax / 句法学 ⋯⋯⋯⋯⋯⋯⋯⋯⋯⋯⋯⋯⋯⋯⋯⋯⋯⋯⋯⋯⋯ 51

Chapter 6
Pragmatics / 语用学 ⋯⋯⋯⋯⋯⋯⋯⋯⋯⋯⋯⋯⋯⋯⋯⋯⋯⋯⋯ 61

Chapter 7
Discourse Analysis / 话语分析 ⋯⋯⋯⋯⋯⋯⋯⋯⋯⋯⋯⋯⋯⋯⋯ 73

Chapter 8
Teaching Methodologies and Testing / 语言教学与测试 ⋯⋯⋯⋯ 79

Chapter 9
Language Acquisition / 语言习得 ⋯⋯⋯⋯⋯⋯⋯⋯⋯⋯⋯⋯⋯ 89

Chapter 10
Cognitive Linguistics / 认知语言学 ⋯⋯⋯⋯⋯⋯⋯⋯⋯⋯⋯⋯ 107

Chapter 11
Language and Culture / 语言与文化 ⋯⋯⋯⋯⋯⋯⋯⋯⋯⋯⋯⋯ 121

Chapter 12
Sociolinguistics / 社会语言学 ·· 141

Chapter 13
Psycholinguistics / 心理语言学 ·· 157

Chapter 14
Neurolinguistics / 神经语言学 ·· 179

Chapter 15
Corpus Linguistics / 语料库语言学 ·· 187

Chapter 16
Stylistics / 文体学 ·· 193

Appendixes ·· 209
Appendix 1　Keys to the Exercises / 练习答案 ························ 209
Appendix 2　A Model Test of Linguistics / 语言学测试题 ············ 233
Appendix 3　A Qualifying Exam for MA Prospects / 考研语言学试题 ···· 236
Appendix 4　A Comprehensive Exam for MA-TESL Candidates /
研究生资格考试试题 ·· 239

Chapter 1
Language and Linguistics
语言和语言学

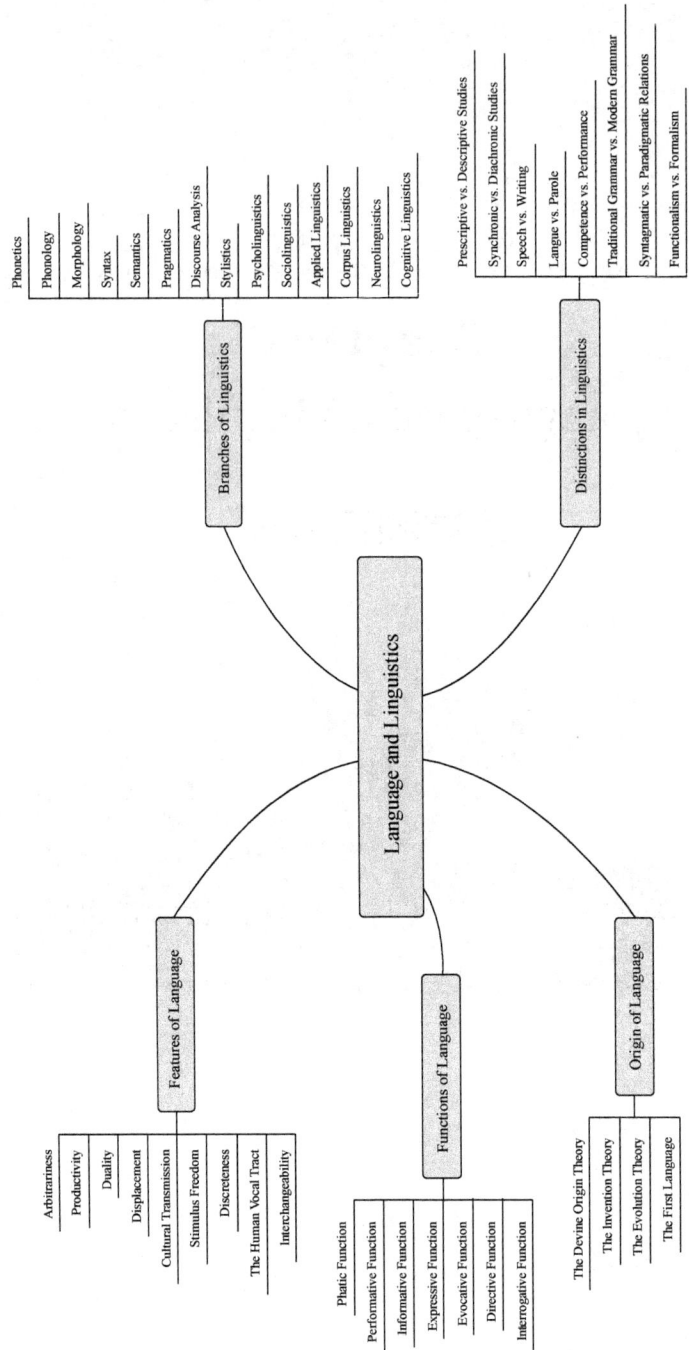

Figure 1 A Mindmap of Language and Linguistics

Chapter 1 Language and Linguistics

> **Key Points**
> Linguistics is generally defined as the scientific study of language. Language is a system of arbitrary vocal symbols used for human communication.

I. Decide whether each of the following statements is true or false.

(　) 1. Competence and performance refer respectively to a language user's underlying knowledge about the system of rules and the actual use of language in concrete situations.

(　) 2. Pragmatics is different from semantics in that pragmatics studies meaning not in isolation, but in context.

(　) 3. In the study of linguistics, hypotheses formed should be based on language facts and checked against the observed facts.

(　) 4. General linguistics is generally the study of language as a whole.

(　) 5. The study of meaning in language is known as semantics.

(　) 6. Modern linguistics is different from traditional grammar.

(　) 7. Most animal communication systems lack the primary level of articulation.

(　) 8. The relation between form and meaning in human language is natural.

(　) 9. The reason for French to use *cheval* and English to use *horse* to refer to the same animal is inexplicable.

(　) 10. Duality is one of the characteristics of human language. It refers to the fact that language has two levels of structures: the system of sounds and the system of meanings.

(　) 11. Syntax is different from morphology in that the former not only studies the morphemes, but also the combination of morphemes into words and words into sentences.

(　) 12. Both semantics and pragmatics study meanings.

(　) 13. Morphology studies how words can be formed to produce meaningful sentences.

(　) 14. The study of the ways in which morphemes can be combined to form words is called morphology.
(　) 15. Modern linguistics is mostly prescriptive, but sometimes descriptive.
(　) 16. General linguistics, which relates itself to the research of other areas, studies the basic concepts, theories, descriptions, models and methods applicable in any linguistic study.
(　) 17. Modern linguistics regards the spoken language as primary, not the written language.
(　) 18. Linguistics is generally defined as the scientific study of language.
(　) 19. Langue is relatively stable and systematic while parole is subject to personal and situational constraints.
(　) 20. A scientific study of language is based on what the linguist thinks.
(　) 21. Social changes can often bring about language changes.
(　) 22. A diachronic study of language is the description of language at some point in time.
(　) 23. Prescriptive linguistics is more popular than descriptive linguistics, because it can tell us how to speak correct language.
(　) 24. Descriptive linguistics is concerned with how languages work, not with how they can be improved.
(　) 25. Halliday's linguistic potential is similar to the notions of parole and performance.
(　) 26. The distinction between competence and performance was proposed by F. de Saussure.
(　) 27. Linguistics studies particular language, not languages in general.
(　) 28. Arbitrariness of language makes it potentially creative, and conventionality of language makes a language be passed from generation to generation. As a foreign language learner, the latter is more important for us.
(　) 29. Phonetics is different from phonology in that the latter studies the combinations of the sounds to convey meaning in communication.

(　) 30. Sociolinguistics is the study of language in relation to society.
(　) 31. By diachronic study we mean to study the changes and development of language.
(　) 32. When language is used to get information from others, it serves an informative function.
(　) 33. Language change is universal, ongoing and arbitrary.
(　) 34. Applied linguistics is the application of linguistic principles and theories to language teaching and learning.

II. Fill in each of the blanks with one word which begins with the letter given.

1. Human capacity for language has a g_____ basis, but the details of language have to be taught and learned.
2. By saying language is arbitrary, we mean that there is no logical connection between meaning and s_____.
3. Langue refers to the a_____ linguistic system shared by all the members of a speech community while the parole is the concrete use of the conventions and application of the rules.
4. Language is p_____ in that it makes possible the construction and interpretation of new signals by its users. In other words, they can produce and understand an infinitely large number of sentences which they have never heard before.
5. Chomsky defines "competence" as the ideal user's k_____ of the rules of his language.
6. Language is a s_____ of arbitrary vocal symbols used for human communication.
7. Findings in linguistic studies can often be applied to the settlement of some practical problems. The study of such applications is generally known as a_____ linguistics.
8. The discipline that studies the rules governing the formation of words into permissible sentences in languages is called s_____.

A Collection of Exercises in Linguistics

9. D_____ is one of the design features of human language which refers to the phenomenon that language consists of two levels: a lower level of meaningless individual sounds and a higher level of meaningful units.
10. In Saussure's view, the relationship between signifier (sound image) and signified (concept) is a_____.
11. Language is a system of a_____ vocal symbols used for human communication.
12. P_____ refers to the realization of langue in actual use.
13. Linguistics is generally defined as the s_____ study of language.

III. Mark the choice that can best complete the statement.

( ) 1. Which of the following is one of the core branches of linguistics?
   A. Phonology.   B. Psycholinguistics.
   C. Sociolinguistics.   D. Anthropology.

( ) 2. Modern linguistics regards the written language as _____.
   A. primary   B. correct   C. secondary   D. stable

( ) 3. The details of any language system are passed on from one generation to the next through _____, rather than by instinct.
   A. learning   B. teaching   C. books   D. both A and B

( ) 4. Which of the following is NOT a design feature of human language?
   A. arbitrariness B. duality   C. displacement   D. diachronicity

( ) 5. Articulatory phonetics mainly studies _____.
   A. the physical properties of the sounds produced in speech
   B. the perception of sounds
   C. the combination of sounds
   D. the production of sounds

( ) 6. Where is the primary stress of the word "phonology"?
   A. pho   B. no   C. lo   D. gy

( ) 7. Language is said to be arbitrary because there is no logical connection between _____ and meanings.
   A. sense   B. sounds   C. objects   D. ideas

(　　) 8. An _____ language is a language in which concepts that we express using prepositions, possessive adjectives, and so on are expressed as morphs concatenated in the same words as the relevant base.

　　A. inflecting　　B. agglutinating　C. isolating　　　D. analytical

(　　) 9. Which of the following branches of linguistics takes the inner structure of word as its main object of study?

　　A. Phonetics　　B. Semantics　　C. Morphology　D. Syntax

(　　) 10. Which of the following groups of words is a minimal pair?

　　A. but–pub　　B. wet–which　　C. cool–curl　　D. fail–find

(　　) 11. _____ is the branch of linguistics which studies the characteristics of speech sounds and provides methods for their description, classification and transcription.

　　A. Phonetics　　B. Phonology　　C. Semantics　　D. Pragmatics

(　　) 12. Where are the vocal cords?

　　A. In the mouth.　　　　　　　B. In the nasal cavity.

　　C. Above the tongue.　　　　　D. Inside the larynx.

(　　) 13. In modern linguistics, speech is regarded as more basic than writing, because _____.

　　A. in linguistic evolution, speech is prior to writing

　　B. speech plays a greater role than writing in terms of the amount of information conveyed

　　C. speech is always the way in which every native speaker acquires his mother tongue

　　D. all of the above

(　　) 14. Which of the following is not one of the criteria of vowel description?

　　A. The part of the tongue that is raised.

　　B. The extent to which the tongue rises.

　　C. The shape of the lips.

　　D. The extent to which the teeth draw together.

( ) 15. The onset of a syllable can be composed of _____.
   A. one vowel   B. two vowels   C. three consonants   D. four consonants

( ) 16. In the following lines "And where are they?" and "where are thou?", the last word "thou" should be stressed because it is in a comparative position with the word "they". We name this kind of sentence stress as _____.
   A. structural sentence stress   B. contrastive sentence stress
   C. grammatical sentence stress   D. primary sentence stress

( ) 17. The distinction between vowels and consonants lies in _____.
   A. the place of articulation   B. the obstruction of airstream
   C. the position of the tongue   D. the shape of the lips

( ) 18. Saussure took a (n) _____ view of language, while Chomsky looks at language from a _____ point of view.
   A. sociological, psychological   B. Psychological, sociological
   C. applied, pragmatic   D. semantic and linguistic

( ) 19. If a linguistic study describes and analyzes the language people actually use, it is said to be _____.
   A. prescriptive   B. analytic
   C. descriptive   D. linguistic

( ) 20. _____ is the defining properties of units like noun (number, gender, etc.) and verb (tense, aspect, etc.).
   A. Parts of speech   B. Word classes linguistic system shared by all
   C. Grammatical categories D. Functions of words

( ) 21. The phonological features of the consonant [k] are _____.
   A. voiced stop   B. voiceless stop
   C. voiced fricative   D. voiceless fricative

( ) 22. Which of the following sounds does not belong to the allomorphs of the English plural morpheme?
   A. /s/   B. /iz/   C. /ai/   D. /is/

( ) 23. Which of the following is not a distinctive feature in English?
   A. voicing   B. nasal   C. approximation   D. aspiration

Chapter 1 Language and Linguistics

( ) 24. Which of the following sounds is a vowel glide?

A. /t/   B. /ɒ/   C. /ei/   D. /ə/

( ) 25. /e/ is different from /a/ in _____.

A. the shape of the lips

B. the height of the tongue

C. the part of the tongue that is raised

D. the position of the soft palate

( ) 26. According to Chomsky, _____ is the ideal user's internalized knowledge of his language.

A. competence   B. parole   C. performance   D. langue

( ) 27. Which of the following features is NOT one of the design features of language?

A. Symbolic   B. Duality   C. Productiveness   D. Arbitrariness

( ) 28. Vibration of the vocal cords results in _____.

A. aspiration   B. nasality   C. obstruction   D. voicing

( ) 29. _____ studies all the speech sounds that human beings produce.

A. Phonetics   B. Phonology   C. Semantics   D. Pragmatics

( ) 30. Which of the following is not a design feature of human language?

A. Arbitrariness.   B. Displacement.

C. Duality.   D. Meaningfulness.

( ) 31. Which of the following statements about language is NOT true?

A. Language is a system.   B. Language is symbolic.

C. Animals also have language.   D. Language is arbitrary.

( ) 32. Language can be used to refer to contexts removed from the immediate situations of the speaker. This feature is called _____.

A. displacement   B. duality

C. flexibility   D. cultural transmission

( ) 33. Which consonant represents the following description: voiceless labiodentals fricative?

A. /v/   B. /s/   C. /f/   D. /m/

( ) 34. What is the most important function of language?
   A. Interpersonal.   B. Phatic.
   C. Informative.   D. Metalingual.

( ) 35. What is the common factor of the three sounds: /p/, /k/, /t/?
   A. Voiceless   B. Spread   C. Voiced   D. Nasal

( ) 36. Usually, suprasegmental features include _____, length and pitch.
   A. phoneme   B. speech sounds   C. syllables   D. stress

( ) 37. Which of the following distinctive features can be used to separate /k/ from /g/?
   A. Glottal (place of articulation)   B. Nasal
   C. Voiced   D. Spread

( ) 38. A historical study of language is a _____ study of language.
   A. synchronic   B. diachronic
   C. prescriptive   D. comparative

( ) 39. According to F. de Saussure, _____ refers to the abstract linguistic system shared by all the members of a speech community.
   A. parole   B. performance
   C. langue   D. language

( ) 40. Which of the following modes of study emphasizes on the "standards" of language?
   A. Prescriptive   B. Descriptive   C. Synchronic   D. Diachronic

( ) 41. The study of language at some point of time is generally termed as _____ linguistics.
   A. applied   B. diachronic   C. comparative   D. synchronic

( ) 42. Who put forward the distinction between Langue and Parole?
   A. Saussure   B. Chomsky   C. Halliday   D. Anonymous

( ) 43. What are the dual structures of language?
   A. Sounds and letters.   B. Sounds and meaning.
   C. Letters and meaning.   D. Sounds and symbols.

( ) 44. /p/ is different from /k/ in _____.
   A. the manner of articulation   B. the shape of the lips
   C. the vibration of the vocal cords   D. the place of articulation
( ) 45. _____ is an indispensable part of a syllable.
   A. Coda   B. Onset   C. Stem   D. Peak
( ) 46. _____ is the study of speech sound in language with reference to their distribution and patterning and to tacit rules governing pronunciation.
   A. Phonology   B. Lexicography   C. Lexicology   D. Morphology
( ) 47. The plural affix in the word *tables* is a(n) _____.
   A. inflectional suffix   B. derivational suffix
   C. free morpheme   D. root
( ) 48. The diphthong in the word *bite* is composed of _____.
   A. /a/ and /i/   B. /e/ and /i/   C. /a/ and /e/   D. /ɒ/ and /i/
( ) 49. What phonetic feature distinguishes the [p] in *please* and the [p] in *speak*?
   A. Voicing   B. Aspiration   C. Roundness   D. Nasality
( ) 50. Minimal pairs are used to _____.
   A. find the distinctive features of a language
   B. find the phonemes of a language
   C. compare two words
   D. find the allophones of a language

IV. Fill in the blank.

1. The design features of language are _____, _____, _____, _____, _____, _____, and _____.
2. Language, broadly speaking, is a means of _____ communication.
3. By duality is meant the property of having two levels of structure, which are _____ level, and _____ level.
4. Consonant sounds can be either _____ or _____, while all vowel sounds are _____.

A Collection of Exercises in Linguistics

5. _____ refers to the phenomenon of sounds continually showing the influence of their neighbors.
6. _____ refer to the defining properties of human language that tell the difference between human language and any system of animal communication.
7. The criteria of consonant description involve the _____ of articulation and the _____ of articulation.
8. _____ studies how speech sounds are made, transmitted, and received, while _____ is the study of the sound systems of languages.
9. _____ means the lack of a logical connection between the form of something and its expression in sounds.
10. _____ function of language refers to the social interaction of language.
11. _____ function of language can be used to talk about itself, and this makes the language infinitely _____.
12. Theory that primitive man made involuntary vocal noises while performing heavy work has been called the _____ theory.
13. _____ means that human languages enable their users to symbolize objects, events and concepts, which are not present in time and space at the moment of communication.
14. Modern linguistics is _____ in the sense that the linguist tries to discover what language is rather than lay down some rules for people to observe.
15. In any language words can be used in new ways to mean new things and can be combined into innumerable sentences based on limited rules. This feature is usually termed _____.
16. Language has many functions. We can use language to talk about itself. This function is _____.
17. If two smallest linguistic units cannot signal a difference in meaning, they are _____.
18. In phonological analysis the words *fail/veil* are distinguishable simply because of the two phonemes /f/ – /v/. This is an example for illustrating _____.
19. Contrastive distribution can be found in _____ pairs.

20. In English there are a number of _____, which are produced by moving from one vowel position to another through intervening positions.
21. A _____ study refers to the study of language at some point of time.
22. If two smallest linguistic units that can signal a difference in meaning, it is _____.
23. Consonants differ from vowels in that the latter are produced without _____.
24. _____ is the smallest linguistic unit.
25. The four sounds /p/, /b/, /m/ and /w/ have one feature in common, i.e. they are all _____.
26. One element in the description of vowels is the part of the tongue which is at the highest point in the mouth. A second element is the _____ to which that part of the tongue is raised.
27. The principal supra-segmental features are _____, _____ and intonation.
28. _____ phonetics studies the movement of the vocal organs of producing the sounds of speech.
29. One general principle of linguistic analysis is the primacy of _____ over writing.
30. The consonant /b/ can be described as a voiced _____ stop.
31. If two sounds never appear in the same position, they are said to be in _____ distribution.
32. The qualities of vowels depend upon the position of the _____ and the lips.
33. A _____ is a complete closure of the articulators so that the airstream cannot escape through the mouth.
34. The description of a language as it changes through time is a _____ study.
35. Saussure put forward two important concepts. _____ refers to the abstract members of a speech community.
36. A syllable must have a _____ or peak, which is usually a _____.

37. If two sounds occurring in the same environment do not contrast, namely, if the substitution of one for the other does not generate a new word form but merely a different pronunciation of the same word, the two sounds then are said to be in _____.

38. Consonant sounds can also be made when two organs of speech in the mouth are brought close together so that the air is pushed out between them, causing _____.

39. Sounds appear in the same environment and the substitution of one by the other result in a change of word meaning are said to be in _____ distribution.

40. The consonant /p/ can be described as a voiceless _____ stop.

41. _____ is defined as the scientific study of language, studying languages in general.

42. The consonant /g/ can be described as a voiced _____ stop.

43. English belongs to _____ language groups.

44. A _____ study refers to the study of language as it changes through time.

45. Linguistics is the _____ study of language.

V. Define the following terms.

design features	syntax	pragmatics
productivity	applied linguistics	psycholinguistics
phonetics	displacement	langue
parole	language	competence
linguistics	phonology	duality
arbitrariness	morphology	semantics
sociolinguistics	performance	

Chapter 1　Language and Linguistics

VI. Answer the following questions as comprehensively as possible. Give examples for illustration if necessary.

1. What characteristics of language do you think should be included in a good, comprehensive definition of language?
2. What are the major distinctions between langue and parole?
3. What are the design features of human language? Illustrate them with examples.
4. How is Saussure's distinction between langue and parole similar to Chomsky's distinction between competence and performance?
5. Point out three ways in which linguistics differs from traditional grammar.
6. Is modern linguistics mainly synchronic or diachronic? Why?
7. Explain speech and writing, and cite two or more examples.
8. What are the major branches of linguistics? What does each of them study?
9. What are the four principles for the scientific study of language?
10. For what reasons does modern linguistics give priority to speech rather than to writing?
11. How do you understand competence and performance?
12. Why does modern linguistics regard the spoken form of language as primary, not the written?
13. What are the major functions of language? Think of your own examples for illustration.
14. Explain the following definition of linguistics: Linguistics is the scientific study of language.
15. Which enjoys priority in modern linguistics, speech or writing? Why?
16. What features of human language have been specified by C. Hockett to show that it is essentially different from any animal communication system?
17. Do you think human language is entirely arbitrary? Why?
18. What makes modern linguistics different from traditional grammar?

19. Saussure's distinction between langue and parole seems similar to Chomsky's distinction between competence and performance. What do you think are their major differences?
20. How do you understand the distinction between a synchronic study and a diachronic study?
21. Define general linguistics and describe its main branches.
22. Language is generally defined as a system of arbitrary vocal symbols used for human communication. Explain it in detail.

Chapter 2
Phonetics and Phonology
语音学和音素学

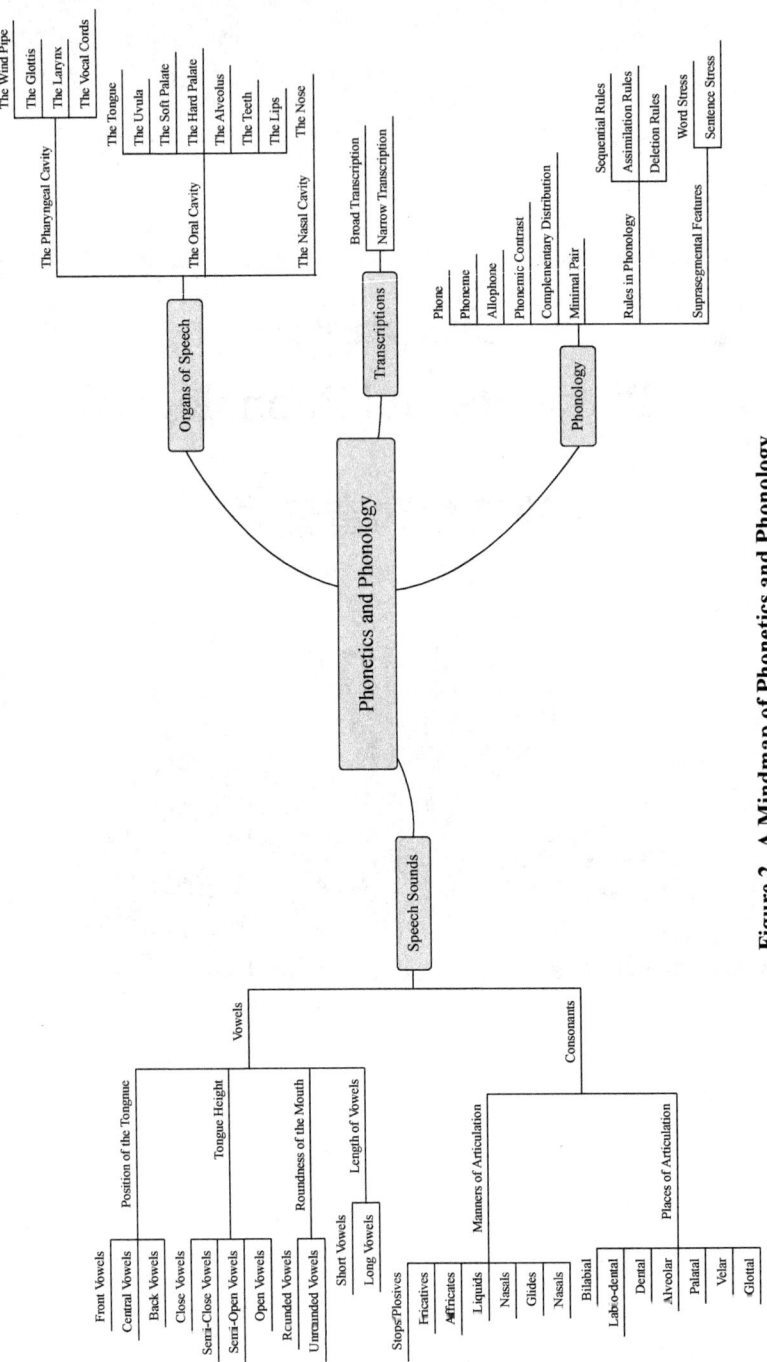

Figure 2 A Mindmap of Phonetics and Phonology

Chapter 2 Phonetics and Phonology

> **Key Points**
> Phonetics is the study of the sounds used in linguistic communication. Phonology is the study of how sounds are put together and used to convey meaning in communication.

I. Decide whether each of the following statements is true or false.

(　) 1. When two different forms are identical in every way except for one sound segment which occurs in the same place in the strings, the two words are said to form a phonemic contrast.

(　) 2. /z/ is the voiced dental fricative.

(　) 3. Of the three phonetics branches, the longest established one, and until recently the most highly developed, is acoustic phonetics.

(　) 4. Distinctive features of sound segments can be found running over a sequence of two or more phonemic segments.

(　) 5. English is a tone language while Chinese is not.

(　) 6. According to the shape of the lips, vowels can be classified into close vowels, semi-close vowels, semi-open vowels and open vowels.

(　) 7. /n/ is one of syllabic consonants.

(　) 8. In linguistic evolution, speech is prior to writing.

(　) 9. Received pronunciation is the pronunciation accepted by most people.

(　) 10. The hard roof of mouth is called hard palate.

(　) 11. The rules governing the phonological patterning are language specific.

(　) 12. The word "film" contains a syllabic consonant.

(　) 13. Broad transcription represents phonemes of a language whereas narrow transcription denotes its particular allophones.

(　) 14. Most animal communication systems lack the primary level of articulation.

(　) 15. Acoustic phonetics is concerned with the perception of speech sounds.

(   ) 16. Phonology is concerned with how the sounds can be classified into different categories.
(   ) 17. The word "hour" contains a diphthong and a pure vowel.
(   ) 18. A basic way to determine the phonemes of a language is to see if substituting one sound for another results in a change of meaning.
(   ) 19. According to the length or tenseness of the pronunciation, vowels can be divided into tense vs. lax or long vs. short.
(   ) 20. Voicing is a phonological feature that distinguishes meaning in both Chinese and English.
(   ) 21. Articulatory phonetics tries to describe the physical properties of the stream of sounds which a speaker issues with the help of a machine called spectrograph.
(   ) 22. When pure or monophthongs are pronounced, no vowel glides take place.
(   ) 23. A phone is a phonetic unit that distinguishes meaning.
(   ) 24. If two phonetically similar sounds occur in the same environments and they distinguish meaning, they are said to be in complementary distribution.
(   ) 25. In everyday communication, speech plays a greater role than writing in terms of the amount of information conveyed.
(   ) 26. The articulatory apparatus of a human being are contained in three important areas: the throat, the mouth and the chest.
(   ) 27. The sound /p/ in the word "expensive" is pronounced as a voiceless consonant.
(   ) 28. Vibration of the vocal cords results in a quality of speech sounds called voicing.
(   ) 29. English consonants can be classified in terms of place of articulation and the part of the tongue that is raised the highest.
(   ) 30. According to the manner of articulation, some of the types into which the consonants can be classified are stops, fricatives, bilabial and alveolar.
(   ) 31. Allophones are described in phonetic terms.

(　) 32. /ɔː/ is a mid-high back rounded vowel.
(　) 33. /p/ is voiced bilabial stop.
(　) 34. A phoneme in one language or one dialect may be an allophone in another language or dialect.
(　) 35. In English, we have the syllable structure of CCCVCCCC.
(　) 36. Sound /p/ in the word "spit" is an unaspirated stop.
(　) 37. The airstream provided by the lungs has to undergo a number of modificaiton to acquire the quality of a speech sound.
(　) 38. Any sound produced by a human being is a phoneme.
(　) 39. In the sound writing system, the reference of the grapheme is the phoneme.
(　) 40. Vowel sounds can be differentiated by a number of factors: the position of tongue in the mouth, the openness of the mouth, the shape of the lips, and the length of the vowels.

II. Mark the choice that can best complete the statement.

(　) 1. Of all the speech organs, the _____ is/are the most flexible.
　　　A. mouth　　　B. lips　　　C. tongue　　　D. vocal cords
(　) 2. The sounds produced without the vocal cords vibrating are _____ sounds.
　　　A. voiceless　　B. voiced　　C. vowel　　　D. consonantal
(　) 3. _____ is a voiced alveolar stop.
　　　A. /z/　　　　B. /d/　　　　C. /k/　　　　D. /b/
(　) 4. The assimilation rule assimilates one sound to another by "copying" a feature of a sequential phoneme, thus making the two phones _____.
　　　A. identical　　B. same　　　C. exactly alike　D. similar
(　) 5. Since /p/ and /b/ are phonetically similar, occur in the same environments and they can distinguish meaning, they are said to be _____.
　　　A. in phonemic contrast　　　B. in complementary distribution
　　　C. the allophones　　　　　　D. minimal pair

A Collection of Exercises in Linguistics

( ) 6. The sound /f/ is _____.
   A. voiced palatal affricate   B. voiced alveolar stop
   C. voiceless velar fricative   D. voiceless labiodental fricative

( ) 7. A _____ vowel is one that is produced with the front part of the tongue maintaining the highest position.
   A. back   B. central   C. front   D. middle

( ) 8. Distinctive features can be found running over a sequence of two or more phonemic segments. The phonemic features that occur above the level of the segments are called _____.
   A. phonetic components   B. immediate constituents
   C. suprasegmental features   D. semantic features

( ) 9. A(n) _____ is a unit that is of distinctive value. It is an abstract unit, a collection of distinctive phonetic features.
   A. phone   B. sound   C. allophone   D. phoneme

( ) 10. The different phones which can represent a phoneme in different phonetic environments are called the _____ of that phoneme.
   A. phones   B. sounds   C. phonemes   D. allophones

( ) 11. Which of the following are speech organs?
   A. lungs   B. trachea   C. kidney   D. vocal folds

( ) 12. When the vocal folds are apart, the air can pass through easily. The sound thus produced is said to be _____.
   A. voiced   B. voiceless   C. aspirated   D. unaspirated

( ) 13. When the vocal folds are totally closed, and no air can pass through them, the resultant sound is the _____.
   A. glottal stop   B. glottal fricative
   C. glottal nasal   D. glottal approximant

( ) 14. According to G. B. Shaw's ridicule of English orthography, the non-existent word *ghoti* can be pronounced in the same way as _____.
   A. goat   B. hot   C. fish   D. foot

Chapter 2　Phonetics and Phonology

(　) 15. The International Phonetic Association was established as the Phonetic Teachers' Association in _____.
A. 1886　　　B. 1986　　　C. 1897　　　D. 1997

(　) 16. Consonants and vowels are distinguished by _____.
A. place of articulation　　　B. manner of articulation
C. obstruction of airflow　　　D. total stopping of air

(　) 17. Which of the following is known as "manner of articulation"?
A. plosive　　B. lateral　　C. stop　　D. bilabial

(　) 18. Which of the following is known as "place of articulation"?
A. velar　　B. affricate　　C. palatal　　D. uvular

(　) 19. Which of the following is the correct description of /b/?
A. voiceless bilabial stop　　　B. voiced bilabial stop
C. voiceless bilabial fricative　　　D. voiced bilabial fricative

(　) 20. Which of the following is the correct description of /k/?
A. voiceless palatal fricative　　　B. voiced velar stop
C. voiced velar fricative　　　D. voiceless velar stop

(　) 21. Which of the following is the correct description of /v/?
A. voiceless labiodental fricative　　　B. voiced labiodental fricative
C. voiceless labiodental stop　　　D. voiced labiodental stop

(　) 22. Which of the following is useful in the description of vowels?
A. place of articulation　　　B. manner of articulation
C. uvular　　　D. height of tongue rise

(　) 23. Which of the following is called *schwa*?
A. /a/　　B. /æ/　　C. /ɒ/　　D. /ə/

(　) 24. Which of the following is described as "close front tense rounded vowel"?
A. /i/　　B. /ɒ/　　C. /e/　　D. /u/

(　) 25. Which of the following is described as "open back unrounded vowel"?
A. /e/　　B. /ɒ/　　C. /u/　　D. /a/

III. Define the following terms.

phonology	phoneme	allophone
intonation	phonetics	auditory phonetics
acoustic phonetics	phone	phonemic contrast
tone	minimal pair	distinctive features
allophone	allomorph	complementarity
morpheme	inflectional morphemes	bound morpheme
backformation	folk etymology	morphology
blending	morphophonemics	morphophonology
root	lexical word	inflection
assimilation	vowels	cardinal vowels
narrow transcription	diphthong	complimentary distribution

IV. Answer the following questions as comprehensively as possible. Give examples for illustration if necessary.

1. Of the two media of language, why do you think speech is more basic than writing?
2. What are the criteria that a linguist uses in classifying vowels?
3. What are the major differences between phonology and phonetics?
4. Illustrate with examples how suprasegmental features can affect meaning.
5. In what way can we determine whether a phone is a phoneme or not?
6. Give the phonetic term for each of the following descriptions.
    (1) the sound produced by the lower lip and the upper front teeth
    (2) the sound produced with a complete closure in the mouth so that the air stream cannot escape through the mouth

7. Identify the manner of articulation of the initial sounds in the following words:
   (1) silly
   (2) crazy
   (3) jolly
   (4) merry
   (5) dizzy
   (6) happy
   (7) loony
   (8) funny
8. Give the correct English symbol for each of the following phonenic feature complexes.
   (1) lateral + velarized
   (2) alveolar + devoice + stop + nasal
   (3) front + high + tense + low
   (4) back + high + tense + lengthened
9. In some dialects of English the following words have different vowels, as shown in the following phonetic transcriptions. State the rule which relates the phonetic representation to the phonetic representations of the words in Columns A, B and C.

A	B	C
bite /bit/	bide /baid/	tie /tai/
rice /ris/	rise /raiz/	by /bai/
type /tip/	bribe /braib/	sigh /sai/
wife /wif/	wives /waivz/	die /dai/
dyke /dik/	time /taim/	tire /tai/

10. Write out the following English words in phonetic notation and show the morphemic breaks with a hyphen, as follows: received /ri-si:v-d/
    (1) abroad
    (2) inducted
    (3) baker
    (4) wishes
    (5) repressed
    (6) unfolding
    (7) goodness
    (8) followers
    (9) foolishness
    (10) internationalization

11. There is one segment that does not belong to the natural class in each of the following groups of speech sounds. You are required to identify that segment and label the natural class, using a descriptive term as specific as possible.
    (1) /m/ /n/ /w/ /ŋ/
    (2) /v/ /θ/ /z/ /ð/ /ʒ/
    (3) /i/ /u/ /y/ /ɒ/ /e/
    (4) /n/ /f/ /l/ /s/ /t/ /d/ /z/
12. Divide the syllables of each of the following English words. Example: discuss: dis+cuss
    (1) pushy: (2) second: (3) punish:
    (4) people: (5) logic: (6) plantation:
13. Which of the following words would be treated as minimal pairs and minimal sets?
    pat   pen   more   heat   tape   bun   fat   ban   chain   tale   bell   far
    meal vote bet   pit   heel   ten   men   put   main   hit   eat   man
14. Each of the following phrases has one letter(s) that is underlined. Write out the phoneme that best records the sound this letter(s) is actually pronounced in spontaneous speech. (Use the International Phonetic Alphabet)
    Example: cotton (c): /k/
    (1) All right (r)   (2) homework (m)
    (3) Good morning (d)   (4) as you may know (s)
    (5) Don't you like me (t)   (6) a meat ball (t)
    (7) Green Park (n)   (8) his telephone call (n)
    (9) ten hooks (n)   (10) Could you go (d)
15. What are the distinctive features that group the following sounds in these sets?
    (1) f, v, s   (2) p, f, b   (3) g, z, b   (4) k, g, w   (5) m, n
16. What is free variation? And illustrate it with examples.
17. Underline the words that contain a sound as required.
    (1) a low vowel: pipe, gather, article, leave, cook
    (2) a bilabial consonant: cool, lad, leap, bomb, push

(3) an approximant: lucky, boots, word, once, table

(4) a front vowel: god, neat, pit, lush, cook

(5) a velar: god, fast, chat, lake, quick

18. Give the phonetic term for each of the following locations in articulation.

    (1) Both lips   (2) Teeth

    (3) Opening between vocal cords   (4) Ridge behind upper teeth

19. What is the difference between a dialect and an accent?

20. What are the contrastive and complementary distributions in the isolation of phonemes? Give examples.

21. Give the phonetic term for each of the following descriptions.

    (1) the sound produced by the lower lip and the upper front teeth

    (2) the sound produced with a complete closure in the mouth so that the air stream cannot escape through the mouth

22. What are the three branches of phonetics? How do they contribute to the study of speech sounds?

23. Where are the articulatory apparatus of a human being contained?

24. What is voicing and how is it caused?

25. What is the function of the nasal cavity? How does it perform this function?

26. Describe the various parts in the oral cavity which are involved in the production of speech sounds?

27. Explain with examples how broad transcription and narrow transcription differ?

28. Give the phonetic symbol for each of the following sound descriptions.

    (1) voiced palatal affricate

    (2) voiceless labiodental fricative

    (3) voiced alveolar stop

    (4) front, close, short

    (5) back, semi-open, long

    (6) voiceless, bilabial stop

29. What is a phone? How is it different from a phoneme? How are allophones related to a phoneme?
30. What is a minimal pair and what is a minimal set? Why is it important to identify the minimal set in a language?

Chapter 3
Morphology

形态学

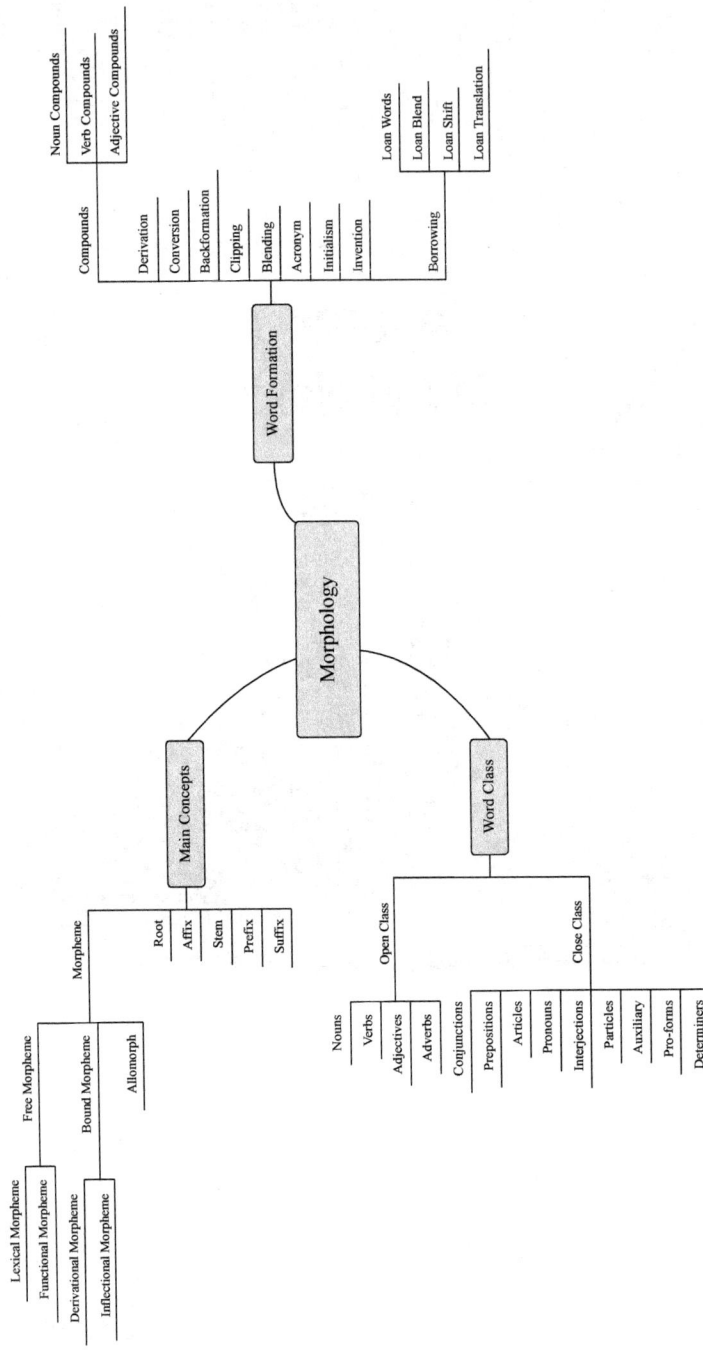

Figure 3 A Mindmap of Morphology

Chapter 3   Morphology

> **Key Points**
> Morphology is the study of the way in which morphemes are arranged to form words.

I. Decide whether each of the following statements is true or false.

( ) 1. Conversion from noun to verb is the most productive process of conversion.

( ) 2. Just as a phoneme is the basic unit in the study of phonology, so is a morpheme the basic unit in the study of morphology.

( ) 3. There are rules that govern which affix can be added to what type of stem to form a new word. Therefore, words formed according to the morphological rules are acceptable words.

( ) 4. Morphology studies the internal structure of words and the rules by which words are formed.

( ) 5. Prefixes usually modify the part of speech of the original word, not the meaning of it.

( ) 6. All bound morphemes are affixes.

( ) 7. Words are the smallest meaningful units of language.

( ) 8. Inflectional morphemes manifest various grammatical relations or grammatical categories such as number, tense, degree, and case.

( ) 9. The smallest meaningful units that can be used freely all by themselves are free morphemes.

( ) 10. Phonetically, the stress of a compound always falls on the first element, while the second element receives secondary stress.

( ) 11. All words contain a root morpheme.

( ) 12. Bound morphemes include two types: roots and affixes.

( ) 13. Base refers to the part of word that remains when all inflectional affixes are removed.

A Collection of Exercises in Linguistics

(　) 14. The words "whimper" "whisper" and "whistle" are formed in the way of onomapoeia.

(　) 15. The existing form to which a derivational affix can be added is called a stem, which can be a bound root, a free morpheme, or a derived form itself.

(　) 16. In most cases, prefixes change the meaning of the base whereas suffixes change the word class of the base.

(　) 17. A root is not always a free form.

(　) 18. Backformation is a productive way of forming nouns in Modern English.

(　) 19. "Plural" is a morpheme.

(　) 20. Phonetically, the stress of a compound always falls on the first element, while the second element receives secondary stress.

(　) 21. All roots are free and all affixes are bound.

(　) 22. Morphemes are regarded as abstract constructs in the system of sound.

(　) 23. Root also falls into two categories: free and bound.

(　) 24. "Fore" as in "foretell" is both a prefix and a bound morpheme.

II. Fill in each of the blanks with one word which begins with the letter given.

1. M_____ is the smallest meaningful unit of language.
2. A s_____ is added to the end of stems to modify the meaning of the original word and it may change its part of speech.
3. D_____ affixes are added to an existing form to create words.
4. The rules that govern which affix can be added to what type of stem to form a new word are called m_____ rules.
5. A s_____ can be a bound root, a free morpheme, or a derived form itself to which a derivational affix can be added.
6. The affix "-ish" in the word boyish conveys a g_____ meaning.
7. B_____ morphemes are those that cannot be used independently but have to be combined with other morphemes, either free or bound, to form a word.

8. Affixes are of two types: inflectional affixes and d_____ affixes.
9. C_____ is the combination of two or sometimes more than two words to create new words.
10. In terms of morphemic analysis, d_____ can be viewed as the addition of affixes to stems to form new words.

III. Mark the choice that can best complete the statement.

(   ) 1. The morpheme "vision" in the common word "television" is a(n) _____.
   A. bound morpheme   B. bound form
   C. inflectional morpheme   D. free morpheme

(   ) 2. _____ belongs to a closed word class.
   A. "In"   B. "Beautiful"   C. "Noun"   D. "Create"

(   ) 3. In the word "conceive", the morpheme "ceive" is a _____.
   A. free root   B. bound root   C. suffix   D. prefix

(   ) 4. The compound word "bookstore" is the place where books are sold. This indicates that the meaning of a compound _____.
   A. is the sum total of the meaning of its components
   B. can always be worked out by looking at the meanings of morphemes
   C. is the same as the meaning of a free phrase
   D. none of the above

(   ) 5. The part of speech of the compounds is generally determined by the part of speech of _____.
   A. the first element
   B. the second element
   C. either the first or the second element
   D. both the first and the second elements

(   ) 6. The meaning carried by the inflectional morpheme is _____.
   A. lexical   B. morphemic   C. grammatical   D. semantic

(   ) 7. Bound morphemes are those that _____.
   A. have to be used independently

B. can not be combined with other morphemes

C. can either be free or bound

D. have to be combined with other morphemes

(　) 8. _____ is a branch of grammar which studies the internal structure of words and the rules by which words are formed.

　　A. Syntax　　B. Grammar　　C. Morphology　　D. Morpheme

(　) 9. The phenomenon that words having different meanings have the same form is called _____.

　　A. hyponymy　　B. synonymy　　C. polysemy　　D. homonymy

(　) 10. The word "lab" is formed through _____.

　　A. back-formation　　B. blending　　C. clipping　　D. derivation

(　) 11. _____ are those that cannot be used independently but have to be combined with other morphemes, either free or bound, to form a word.

　　A. Free morphemes　　　　B. Bound morphemes

　　C. Bound words　　　　　　D. Words

(　) 12. _____ modify the meaning of the stem, but usually do not change the part of speech of the original word.

　　A. Prefixes　　B. Suffixes　　C. Roots　　D. Affixes

(　) 13. _____ are often thought to be the smallest meaningful units of language by the linguists.

　　A. Words　　B. Morphemes　　C. Phonemes　　D. Sentences

(　) 14. "-s" in the word "books" is _____.

　　A. a derivative affix　　B. a stem　　C. an inflectional affix　　D. a root

(　) 15. Which of the following words is created through the process of acronym?

　　A. ad　　B. edit　　C. AIDS　　D. Bobo

IV. Fill in the blanks.

1. Morpheme is the smallest unit of language in terms of relationship between _____ and _____.

2. Words like _____, _____ are created through the process of acronym.

3. _____ are words derived from the initials of several words.
4. _____ morphemes are those that cannot be used independently but have to be combined with other morphemes, either free or bound, to form a word.
5. The affix "-ish" in the word "boyish" conveys a _____ meaning.
6. _____ is the smallest meaningful unit of language.
7. The smallest unit of sound is _____ and the smallest unit in grammar is _____.

V. Define the following terms.

morphology	inflectional morphology	derivational morphology
morpheme	free morpheme	bound morpheme
root	affix	prefix
suffix	derivation	compounding
inflectional morpheme	back-formation	folk etymology
blending	morphophonemics	lexical word
closed-class words	open-class words	inflection
clipping	morphophonology	

VI. Answer the following questions.

1. What are the main features of the English compounds?
2. Discuss the types of morphemes with examples.
3. The component morphs of the following morphologically complex words have been separated by a hyphen (-). Indicate which of these morphs are bound morphs and which are free morphs, and which of the bound morphs are inflectional and which derivational.

   Example: hit-s

       hit: free

       -s: bound, inflectional

   (1) en-courage-ment
   (2) king-dom-s

A Collection of Exercises in Linguistics

(3) stud-ent-hood

(4) anti-soviet-ism

(5) bi-annu-al-ly

(6) read-ing-s

4. Below is a list of acronyms/initialisms. Provide original words for as many of these acronyms/initialisms as you can.

UNICEF	OPEC	MADD	AIDS	NATO
CIA	UNESCO	PLA	PRC	LASER

5. The following quotation is from a *San Francisco Chronicle* opinion piece regarding educational issues by Debra J. Saunders (July 18, 1994):

Politicians and bureaucrats who ignore parents' democratic—small d—rush on this educrats' Tiananmen Square may find themselves on the wrong side of a populist rebellion.

(1) What is an educrat?

(2) What kind of word is educrat? That is, how was it formed?

6. English has two prefixes un-, one is like *untrue, unnatural*, the other is like *untie, undress, unfold*. Now consider the word *unlockable*. If you think about this word long enough, you will realize that it has two different meanings. Show how these two different meanings are in part determined by the fact that English has two different prefixes un-.

7. Consider the word *uninstaller*. Answer the following questions:

(1) Which *un*-prefix is involved? Defend your answer.

(2) What is the structure of *uninstaller*? That is, which affix attaches first, *un*- or *-er*? Defend your answer.

8. Please identify the word formation process involved in producing the italicized forms in these sentences.

(1) Laura *parties* Saturday night.

(2) Tom was worried that he might have *AIDS*.

(3) Zee described the new toy as *fantabulous*.

(4) Eliza exclaimed, "*Absoloominglultely!*"

9. Identify the functional morphemes in the following sentence.

    The old man sat on a chair and told them tales of woe.

10. Identify in the following sentence four bound morphemes. State whether each is derivational or inflectional.

    The teacher's sister considered the project impossible.

11. The use of plural -s in English has three different forms, but very regular phonological alternatives. You add:

    /s/ to wouds like lip, cat, book, and cough

    /z/ to words like cab, bed, rug, and willow

    /iz/ to words like ash, bench, case and bridges

    Work out the set of sounds which regularly precedes each of these alternatives.

12. Try to find out the meaning of the following roots in English and give two or three words that contain each of them.

hydro	chron	demo	dur	agr	kilo
nym	ped	rupt	gress	poly	syn

13. What word-formation processes are involved in the creation of the italicized forms?

    (1) *SARS* is an epidemic which affects our lungs.

    (2) The negotiators *blueprinted* a new peace proposal.

14. Illustrate the difference between root and stem.

15. What are the methods for the addition of new words in the English language?

16. Language can change through blending, metanalysis and borrowing. Give two English words to illustrate each of them.

17. Divide the following words into Roots, Inflectional Affix and/or Derivational Affix.

    (1) transformations   (2) looseleaves   (3) destructive   (4) geese   (5) misled

18. What is a morpheme? Dissect the following words into morphemes.

description	underdeveloped	photosynthetic	anatomy
radiationgeography	philharmonic	defrosted	refreshment
demobilized	conducting	suppression	circumspect
dialogue	deformed	combination	

19. Describe with examples the various types of morpheme used in English.
20. What are the main inflectional affixes in English? What grammatical meaning do they convey?

Chapter 4
Semantics

语义学

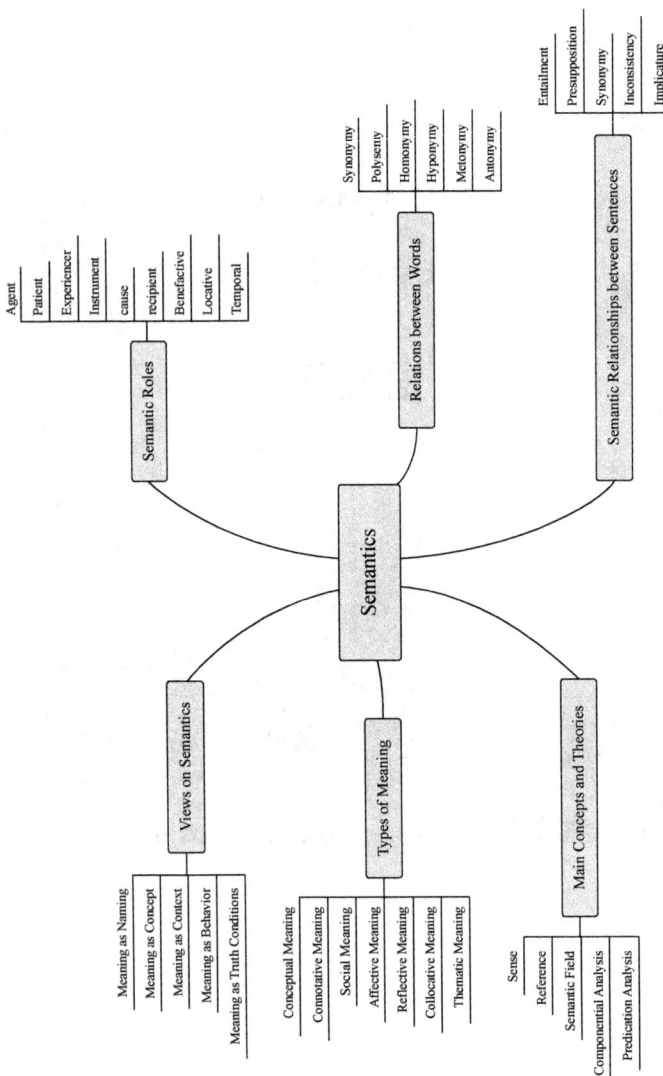

Figure 4 A Mindmap of Semantics

Chapter 4 Semantics

> **Key Points**
> Semantics is the study of linguistic meaning: the meaning of words, phrases, and sentences.

Ⅰ. Decide whether each of the following statements is true or false.

(　) 1. Dialectal synonyms can often be found in different regional dialects such as British English and American English but cannot be found within the variety itself, for example, within British English or American English.

(　) 2. Sense is concerned with the relationship between the linguistic element and the non-linguistic world of experience, while the reference deals with the inherent meaning of the linguistic form.

(　) 3. Linguistic forms having the same sense may have different references in different situations.

(　) 4. In semantics, meaning of language is considered as the intrinsic and inherent relation to the physical world of experience.

(　) 5. Contextualism is based on the presumption that one can derive meaning from or reduce meaning to observable contexts.

(　) 6. Behaviorists attempted to define the meaning of a language form as the situation in which the speaker utters it and the response it calls forth in the hearer.

(　) 7. The meaning of a sentence is the sum total of the meanings of all its components.

(　) 8. Most languages have sets of lexical items similar in meaning but ranked differently according to their degree of formality.

(　) 9. "It is hot." is a no-place predication because it contains no argument.

(　) 10. Two sentences using the same words may mean quite differently.

( ) 11. Linguistic forms having the same sense may have different references in different situations while linguistic forms with the same reference always have the same sense.
( ) 12. "Tulip" "rose" and "violet" are all included in the notion of "flower", therefore they are superordinates of "flower".
( ) 13. The theory of meaning which relates the meaning of a word to the thing it refers to, or stands for, is known as the referential theory.
( ) 14. The relation between form and meaning in human language is natural.
( ) 15. The meaning relationship between MAN and GROWN-UP is hyponymous because the semantic features of MAN are included in those of GROWN-UP.
( ) 16. Semantically, BEEF is excluded in MEAT.
( ) 17. Interrogative and imperative sentences do not have truth value.
( ) 18. Predication of a sentence is identical to the proposition of the sentence.
( ) 19. Greek does not belong to Indo-European Language Family.
( ) 20. After comparing "They stopped at the end of the corridor" with "At the end of the corridor, they stopped", you may find some differences in meaning, and the difference can be interpreted in terms of collocative meaning.
( ) 21. "Kids" and "children" are synonyms despite their stylistic difference.
( ) 22. In the semantic triangle, there is no direct relationship between symbol and referent.
( ) 23. One merit of componential analysis is that by specifying the semantic features of certain words, it will be possible to show how these words are related in meaning.
( ) 24. Hyponymy is a matter of class membership, so it is the same as metonymy.
( ) 25. If a word has sense, it must have reference.
( ) 26. Predication of a sentence is identical to the proposition of the sentence.
( ) 27. The relationship between "human body" and "face/nose" is hyponymy.

( ) 28. Componential analysis is based on the belief that the meaning of a word cannot be dissected into meaning components, called semantic features.
( ) 29. The reason for French to use *cheval* and for English to use *horse* to refer to the same animal is inexplicable.

II. **Fill in each of the following blanks with one word which begins with the letter given.**

1. S_____ can be defined as the study of meaning.
2. The conceptualist view holds that there is no d_____ link between a linguistic form and what it refers to.
3. R_____ means what a linguistic form refers to in the real, physical world; it deals with the relationship between the linguistic element and the non-linguistic world of experience.
4. Words that are close in meaning are called s_____.
5. When two words are identical in sound, but different in spelling and meaning, they are called h_____.
6. R_____ opposites are pairs of words that exhibit the reversal of a relationship between the two items.
7. C_____ analysis is based upon the belief that the meaning of a word can be divided into meaning components.
8. Whether a sentence is semantically meaningful is governed by rules called s_____ restrictions, which are constraints on what lexical items can go with what others.
9. An a_____ is a logical participant in a predication, largely identical with the nominal element (s) in a sentence.
10. According to the n_____ theory of meaning, the words in a language are taken to be labels of the objects they stand for.

III. **Mark the choice that can best complete the statement.**

( ) 1. Semantics can be defined as the study of _____.
   A. words   B. meaning   C. communication   D. context

( ) 2. Sense relates to the complex system of relationships that hold between the linguistic elements themselves (mostly words); it is concerned with _____ relations.
   A. extra-linguistic   B. intra-linguistic
   C. non-linguistic   D. multi-linguistic

( ) 3. Reference deals with the relationship between the linguistic elements (words, sentences, etc) and the _____ world of experience.
   A. extra-linguistic   B. intra-linguistic
   C. non-linguistic   D. multi-linguistic

( ) 4. Two words that are opposite in meaning are called _____.
   A. synonyms   B. homonyms   C. antonyms   D. homophones

( ) 5. The pair of words "wide/narrow" are called _____.
   A. gradable opposites   B. complementary antonyms
   C. co-hyponyms   D. relational opposites

( ) 6. The naming theory is advanced by _____.
   A. Plato   B. Bloomfield   C. Geoffrey Leech   D. Firth

( ) 7. "We shall know a word by the company it keeps." This statement represents _____.
   A. the conceptualist view   B. contexutalism
   C. the naming theory   D. behaviorism

( ) 8. Which of the following is not true?
   A. Sense is concerned with the inherent meaning of the linguistic form.
   B. Sense is the collection of all the features of the linguistic form.
   C. Sense is abstract and de-contextualized.
   D. Sense is the aspect of meaning dictionary compilers are not interested in.

( ) 9. "Can I borrow your bike?" _____ "You have a bike."
   A. is synonymous with   B. is inconsistent with
   C. entails   D. presupposes

( ) 10. _____ is a way in which the meaning of a word can be dissected into meaning components, called semantic features.
   A. Predication analysis   B. Componential analysis
   C. Phonemic analysis   D. Grammatical analysis

( ) 11. What is the meaning relationship between the two words "flower/rose"?
   A. Polysemy   B. Synonymy   C. Hyponymy   D. Antonymy

( ) 12. The words "railway" and "railroad" are _____.
   A. emotive synonyms   B. dialectal synonyms
   C. stylistic synonyms   D. collocational synonyms

( ) 13. The same word may have more than one meaning, which is called _____.
   A. synonymy   B. homonymy   C. hyponymy   D. polysemy

( ) 14. The pair of words "lend" and "borrow" are _____.
   A. gradable antonyms   B. relational opposites
   C. complementary antonyms   D. none of the above

( ) 15. The way to analyze sentence meaning is called _____ analysis.
   A. componential   B. predication   C. syntactic   D. logical

( ) 16. "Alive" and "dead" are _____.
   A. gradable antonyms   B. relational opposites
   C. complementary antonyms   D. none of the above

( ) 17. _____ deals with the relationship between the linguistic element and the non-linguistic world of experience.
   A. Reference   B. Concept   C. Semantics   D. Sense

( ) 18. _____ refers to the phenomenon that words having different meanings have the same form.
   A. Polysemy   B. Synonymy   C. Homonymy   D. Hyponymy

(　) 19. Words that are close in meaning are called _____.
   A. homonyms   B. polysemy   C. hyponyms   D. synonyms
(　) 20. The grammaticality of a sentence is governed by _____.
   A. grammatical rules   B. selectional restrictions
   C. semantic rules   D. semantic features

IV. Define the following terms.

semantics	proposition	predicate logic
metonymy	predication analysis	polysemy
hyponymy	sense	reference
componential analysis	gradable antonyms	selection restriction
synonymy	adjacency pair	idiolect
sociolect	Indo-European family	

V. Answer the following questions.

1. Why do we say that a meaning of a sentence is not the sum total of the meanings of all its components?
2. How do you account for such sense relations between sentences as synonymous relation, inconsistent relation in terms of truth values?
3. According to the way synonyms differ, how many groups can we classify synonyms into? Illustrate them with examples.
4. What are the major views concerning the study of meaning? How they differ?
5. Distinguish between the two possible meanings of more beautiful flowers by means of IC analysis.
6. Classify the following pairs of antonyms into the three types such as complementary, gradable, and converse.
   host–guest   borrow–lend   innocent–guilty   strong–weak
7. Tell the sense relation between A and B in each pair.
   (1) A: She got a tulip. B: She got a flower.

(2) A: You haven't returned the book to me. B: You received a book from me.

(3) A: The boy chased the dog.   B: The dog was chased by the boy.

8. Describe the oddness of the following sentence, using semantic features.

    (1) The television drank my water.

    (2) His dog writes poetry.

9. Identify the semantic roles of all the noun phrases in this sentence.

    With his new golf club, Fred whacked the ball from the words to the grassy area near the river and he felt good.

10. In what way are the following two sentences ambiguous? Please explain with tree diagrams and Chinese translation for each interpretation.

    (1) I shot an elephant in my pajamas this morning.

    (2) This will make you smart.

11. How do you distinguish between homonyms and polysemic lexemes? Give an example of the practical relevance of this distinction.

12. What is Componential Analysis (CA)? Use CA to tell the relation between the words "boy" and "girl".

13. What are the three semantic changes in historical linguistics? Give examples to support your point.

14. What relationship do they have between each other?

    (1) tree–maple, birch   (2) flour–flower

    (3) lend–borrow   (4) male–female

    (5) big–small

15. Put the following words in a hierarchical order (you can use a tree diagram if needed) and try to define at least two of them: crocodile, mammal, reptile, rabbit, primate, animal

16. What are the possible colours of Chinese " 青 " in English? And what does this reflect in semantics?

17. Please give two examples of two-place predicates.

18. Analyze hyponymy and incompatibility by using componential analysis.

19. What are selection restrictions?

A Collection of Exercises in Linguistics

20. Explain the referential theory of meaning, and give examples to support your points.
21. Explain the semantic ambiguity of the following sentences by providing two or more sentences that paraphrase the multiple meanings. Example: "She can't bear children" can mean either "She can't give birth to children" or "She can't tolerate children."
    (1) He waited by the bank.
    (2) Is he really that kind?
    (3) We bought her dog biscuits.
    (4) He saw that gasoline can explode.
    (5) Fifty soldiers shot three wild foxes.
    (6) He saw her drawing pencils.
22. The Encyclopedia Britannica Yearbook has usually published a new word list, which is, in the Britannica's editor's view, a list of those words that had entered the language during the year. Would you expect a yearbook to publish a "lost-word list" recording the words dropped from that language during the year? Defend your answer.
23. Identify which of the following may be considered to have or to be homographs, homophones, homonyms or polysemy:
    sea   break   line   ear   prayer   mature   trace   house
24. What is sense and what is reference? How are they related?
25. What are the major types of synonyms in English?
26. Explain with examples "homonymy" "polysemy" and "hyponymy".
27. How can words opposite in meaning be classified? To which category does each of the following pairs of antonyms belong?
    left–right   far–near   vacant–occupied   father–daughter
    north–south   doctor–patient   dark–bright   ugly–beautiful
28. Identify the relations between the following pairs sentences.
    (1) Tom's wife is pregnant.
        Tom has a wife.

(2) He likes swimming.

　　He likes sports.

(3) My sister will soon be divorced.

　　My sister is a married woman.

(4) He speaks English.

　　He speaks a foreign language.

29. In what way is componential analysis similar to the analysis of phonemes into distinctive features?
30. What is grammaticality? What might make a grammatically meaningful sentence semantically meaningless?
31. Try to analyze the following sentences in terms of predication analysis.

    (1) The man sells ice-cream.

    (2) Is the baby sleeping?

    (3) It is snowing.

    (4) The tree grows well.

32. How do you distinguish between entailment and presupposition in terms of truth values?

Chapter 5
Syntax

句法学

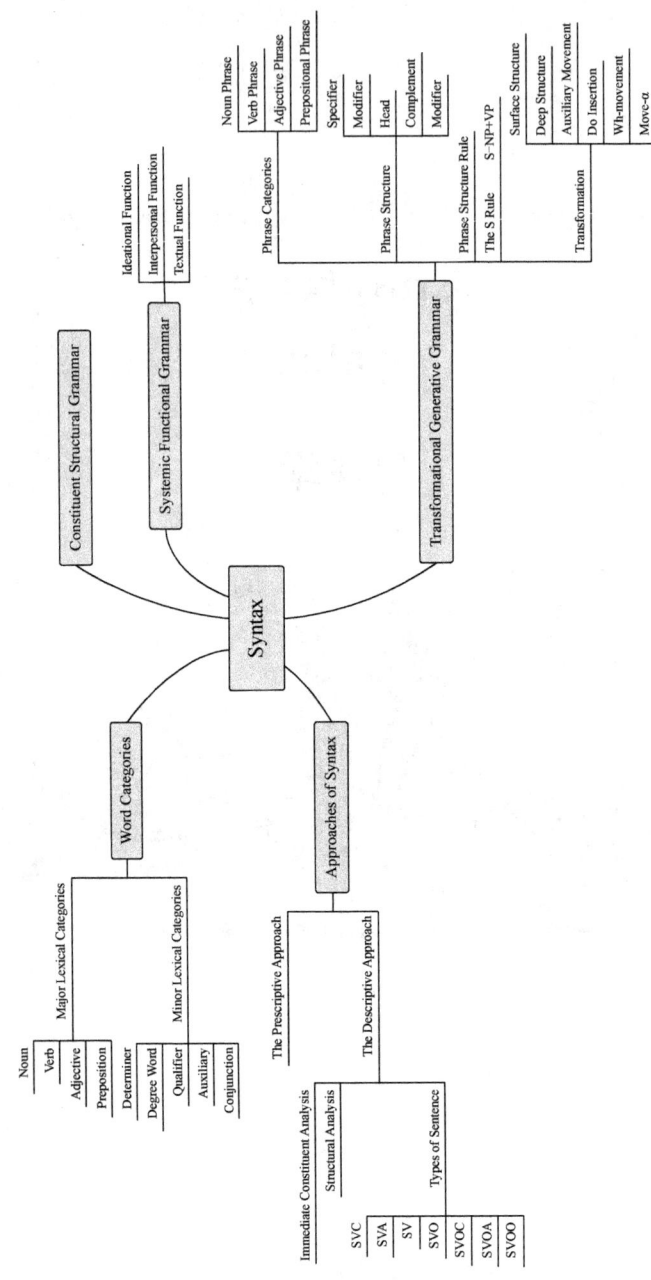

Figure 5 A Mindmap of Syntax

Chapter 5 Syntax

> **Key Points**
> Syntax is the study of those rules that govern the combination of words to form permissible sentences.

I. Decide whether each of the following statements is true or false.

(   ) 1. Syntax is a subfield of linguistics that studies the sentence structure of language, including the combination of morphemes into words.

(   ) 2. Grammatical sentences are formed following a set of syntactic rules.

(   ) 3. Sentences are composed of sequence of words arranged in a simple linear order, with one adding onto another following a simple arithmetic logic.

(   ) 4. Universally found in the grammars of all human languages, syntactic rules that comprise the system of internalized linguistic knowledge of a language speaker are known as linguistic competence.

(   ) 5. The syntactic rules of any language are finite in number, but there is no limit to the number of sentences native speakers of that language are able to produce and comprehend.

(   ) 6. In a complex sentence, the two clauses hold unequal status, one subordinating the other.

(   ) 7. Constituents that can be substituted for one another without loss of grammaticality belong to the same syntactic category.

(   ) 8. Minor lexical categories are open because these categories are not fixed and new members are allowed for.

(   ) 9. In English syntactic analysis, four phrasal categories are commonly recognized and discussed, namely, noun phrase, verb phrase, infinitive phrase, and auxiliary phrase.

(   ) 10. In English the subject usually precedes the verb and the direct object usually follows the verb.

(　　) 11. What is actually internalized in the mind of a native speaker is a complete list of words and phrases rather than grammatical knowledge.

(　　) 12. A noun phrase must contain a noun, but other elements are optional.

(　　) 13. It is believed that phrase structure rules, with the insertion of the lexicon, generate sentences at the level of D-structure.

(　　) 14. Wh-movement is obligatory in English which changes a sentence from affirmative to interrogative.

(　　) 15. Paradigmatic relation in syntax is alternatively called horizontal relation.

(　　) 16. Application of the transformational rules yields deep structure.

(　　) 17. Move-α rule itself can rule out ungrammatical forms and result in grammatical strings.

(　　) 18. Number and gender are categories of noun and pronoun.

(　　) 19. A constituent which is not at the same time a construction is a morpheme, and a construction which is not at the same time a constituent is a sentence.

(　　) 20. IC analysis can be used to analyze all kinds of ambiguous structures.

(　　) 21. A sentence contains a point of departure and a goal of discourse.

(　　) 22. Syntactic category refers to all phrasal syntactic categories such as NP, VP, and PP, and word-level syntactic categories that serve as heads of phrasal syntactic categories such as N and V.

(　　) 23. S-structure is a level of syntactic representation after the operation of necessary syntactic movement.

II. Fill in each of the following blanks with one word which begins with the letter given.

1. A s_____ sentence consists of a single clause which contains a subject and a predicate and stands alone as its own sentence.

2. A s_____ is a structurally independent unit that usually comprises a number of words to form a complete statement, question or command.

3. A s_____ may be a noun or a noun phrase in a sentence that usually precedes the predicate.
4. The part of a sentence which comprises a finite verb or a verb phrase and which says something about the subject is grammatically called p_____.
5. A c_____ sentence contains two, or more, clauses, one of which is incorporated into the other.
6. In the complex sentence, the incorporated or subordinate clause is normally called an e_____ clause.
7. Major lexical categories are o_____ categories in the sense that new words are constantly added.
8. A_____ Condition on case assignment states that a case assignor and a case recipient should stay adjacent to each other.
9. P_____ are syntactic options of UG that allow general principles to operate in one way or another and contribute to significant linguistic variations between and among natural languages.
10. The theory of c_____ condiction explains the fact that noun phrases appear only in subject and object positions.

III. Mark the choice that can best complete the statement.

( ) 1. A sentence is considered _____ when it does not conform to the grammatical knowledge in the mind of native speakers.
  A. right   B. wrong   C. grammatical   D. ungrammatical

( ) 2. A _____ in the embedded clause refers to the introductory word that introduces the embedded clause.
  A. coordinator   B. particle   C. preposition   D. subordinator

( ) 3. Phrase structure rules have _____ properties.
  A. recursive   B. grammatical   C. social   D. functional

(   ) 4. Phrase structure rules allow us to better understand _____.
    A. how words and phrases form sentences
    B. what constitutes the grammaticality of strings of words
    C. how people produce and recognize possible sentences
    D. all of the above

(   ) 5. Syntactic movement is dictated by rules traditionally called _____.
    A. transformational rules   B. generative rules
    C. phrase structure rules   D. X-bar theory

(   ) 6. The theory of case condition accounts for the fact that _____.
    A. noun phrases appear only in subject and object positions
    B. noun phrases can be used to modify another noun phrase
    C. noun phrase can be used in adverbial positions
    D. noun phrase can be moved to any place if necessary

(   ) 7. The sentence structure is _____.
    A. only linear   B. only hierarchical
    C. complex   D. both linear and hierarchical

(   ) 8. The syntactic rules of any language are _____ in number.
    A. large   B. small   C. finite   D. infinite

(   ) 9. The _____ rules are the rules that group words and phrases to form grammatical sentences.
    A. lexical   B. morphological   C. linguistic   D. combinational

(   ) 10. _____ rules may change the syntactic representation of a sentence.
    A. Generative   B. Transformational
    C. X-bar   D. Phrase structure

IV. **Define the following terms.**

paradigmatic relations	phrase structure rules	deep structure
discontinuous constituent	constituent	ultimate constituent
syntagmatic relation	endocentric construction	exocentric construction

transformational rules	government	syntax
sentence	coordinate sentence	syntactic categorie
grammatical relations	linguistic competence	immediate constituent analysis
transformational-generative grammar		

V. Answer the following questions.

1. What are the basic components of a sentence?
2. What are the major types of sentences? Illustrate them with examples.
3. Are the elements in a sentence linearly structured? Why?
4. What are the advantages of using tree diagrams in the analysis of sentence structures?
5. What is NP movement? Illustrate it with examples.
6. Provide the tree diagrams for the following sentences.
   (1) She has finally found the man who loves her.
   (2) The boy repairs the bicycle in the house.
   (3) The dog bit the man in the car.
   (4) The fact that he is a pickpocket is denied by him.
   (5) Jane likes the coat that John bought for the one he loves.
7. Why does Bloomfield theory of syntax use the notion of form classes instead of words?
8. Discuss the merits and limitations of a family tree diagram as a means of representing the synchronic and diachronic relationship between languages.
9. One kind of substitution is the movement of an NP to an empty NP position, which is known as NP movement. Can you show by tree diagrams how the movement rule is realized in the sentence "John seems to be happy."?
10. What syntactic rule is involved in the transformation of the sentence "The man was cheated."? Explain by using tree diagrams.

A Collection of Exercises in Linguistics

11. Paraphrase each of the following sentences in two different ways to show that you understand the ambiguity involved:

    Example: Smoking grass can be nauseating.

    → Putting grass in a pipe and smoking it can make you sick.

    → Fumes from smoldering grass can make you sick.

    (1) Terry loves his wife and so do I.

    (2) They said she would go yesterday.

    (3) The governor is a dirty street fighter.

    (4) The design has big squares and circles.

12. Tell whether each of the underlined part is endocentric or exocentric.

    a matter of degree   the man who laughed

    it is going to take place   the train arrived on time

13. Disambiguate the following sentences, using the tree diagram with labels or analyzing their syntactic structures.

    (1) Leave the book on the shelf.

    (2) my small child's cot (three way ambiguity)

    (3) The son of Pharaoh's daughter is the daughter of the Pharaoh's son.

    (4) Please make her dress fast.

    (5) There are thirty odd teachers in our department.

    (6) The dog she bought likes young children.

14. Tell if each of the following is endocentric or exocentric construction.

    take a break   an extremely difficult book   Ladies and Gentlemen

    at present   swimming in the lake

15. Examine each of the following sentences and indicate if it is a simple, coordinate, or complex sentence.

    (1) Jane did it because she was asked to.

    (2) The soldiers were warned to remain hidden and not to expose themselves.

    (3) David was never there, but his brother was.

    (4) She leads a tranquil life in the country.

    (5) Unless I hear from her, I won't leave this town.

16. Use the appropriate phrase structure rules to draw a labeled constituent structure tree diagram for each of the following sentences.
    (1) A clever magician fooled the audience.
    (2) The tower on the hill collapsed in the wind.
    (3) They knew that the senator would win the election.
17. The formation of many sentences involves the operation of syntactic movement. The following sentences are believed to have derived from their D-structure representations. Show the D-structure for each of these sentences.
    (1) The leader of the majority party was severely criticized by the media.
    (2) The man threw the rake away in the yard.
    (3) Will the new shop owner hire her?
    (4) What can the robot do for us?
18. Draw on your linguistic knowledge of English and paraphrase each of the following sentences in two different ways to show how syntactic rules account for the ambiguity of sentences.
    (1) Tony is a dirty street fighter.
    (2) After a two-day debate, they finally decided on the helicopter.
    (3) The man is too heavy to move.
    (4) The little girl saw the big man with the telescope.
19. Because languages have recursive properties, there is no limit to the potential length of sentences, and the set of sentences of any language is infinite. Give two examples to show the recursive properties of sentences.

Chapter 6
Pragmatics
语用学

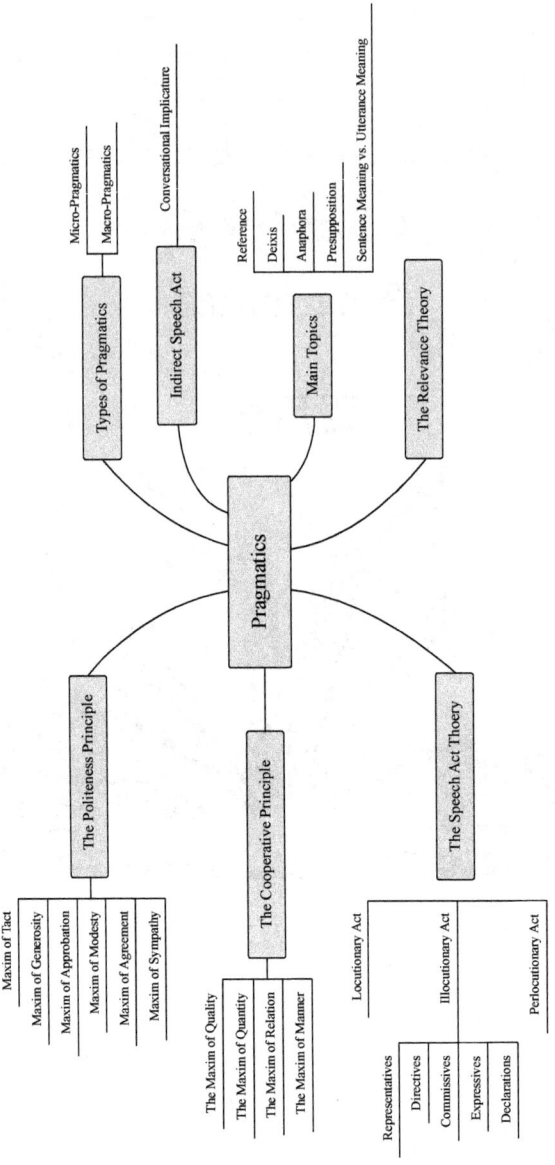

Figure 6 A Mindmap of Pragmatics

Chapter 6 Pragmatics

> **Key Points**
> Pragmatics is the study of how speakers of a language use sentences to effect successful communication.

I. Decide whether each of the following statements is true or false.

(　) 1. Both semantics and pragmatics study how speakers of a language use sentences to effect successful communication.

(　) 2. Pragmatics treats the meaning of language as something intrinsic and inherent.

(　) 3. It would be impossible to give an adequate description of meaning if the context of language use was left unconsidered.

(　) 4. What essentially distinguishes semantics and pragmatics is whether in the study of meaning the context of use is considered.

(　) 5. The major difference between a sentence and an utterance is that a sentence is not uttered while an utterance is.

(　) 6. The meaning of a sentence is abstract, but context-dependent.

(　) 7. The meaning of an utterance is decontexualized, therefore stable.

(　) 8. Utterances always take the form of complete sentences.

(　) 9. Speech act theory was originated with the British philosopher John Searle.

(　) 10. Speech act theory started in the late 50's of the 20th century.

(　) 11. Austin made the distinction between a constative and a performative.

(　) 12. Perlocutionary act is the act of expressing the speaker's intention.

(　) 13. In the following pair of sentences, sentence (b) presupposes sentence (a): (a) John managed to finish in time. (b) John tried to finish in time.

(　) 14. The Cooperative Principle, an important pragmatic principle proposed by P. Grice, aims to explain how we mean more than we say.

(　) 15. A sentence is a grammatical unit and an utterance is a pragmatic notion.

(　) 16. According to Searle's classification of speech acts, *request*, *order*, *suggest* and *advice* all belong to the same one general class because they are all intended by the speaker to get the hearer to do something.
(　) 17. Pragmatics is by and large complementary with semantics.
(　) 18. One performative verb may be performing the type of act suggested by another performative verb.
(　) 19. All words can be used to convey conversational implicatures.
(　) 20. Whenever one fails to fulfill a conversational maxim, one fails to observe the Cooperative Principle altogether.
(　) 21. The more indirect the utterance is to express the speaker's intention, the greater politeness the speaker shows to the hearer.
(　) 22. If the context of use is considered, the study is being carried out in the area of pragmatics.
(　) 23. A locutionary act is the act of expressing the speaker's intention.
(　) 24. When performing an illocutionary act of representative, the speaker is making a statement or giving a description which he himself believes to be true.
(　) 25. The utterance meaning of the sentence varies with the context in which it is uttered.
(　) 26. While conversation participants nearly always observe the CP, they do not always observe these maxims strictly.
(　) 27. Inviting, suggesting, warning, ordering are instances of commissives.
(　) 28. Only when a maxim under Cooperative Principle is blatantly violated and the hearer knows that it is being violated do conversational implications arise.
(　) 29. Of three speech acts, linguists are most interested in the illocutionary act because this kind of speech is identical with the speaker's intention.

II. Fill in each of the blank with one word which begins with the letter given.

1. P_____ is the study of how speakers of a language use sentences to effect successful communication.

2. What essentially distinguishes s_____ and pragmatics is whether in the study of meaning the context of use is considered.
3. The notion of c_____ is essential to the pragmatic study of language.
4. If we think of a sentence as what people actually utter in the course of communication, it becomes an u_____.
5. The meaning of a sentence is a_____, and decontexualized.
6. C_____ were statements that either state or describe, and were thus verifiable.
7. P_____ were sentences that did not state a fact or describe a state, and were not verifiable.
8. A l_____ act is the act of uttering words, phrases, clauses. It is the act of conveying literal meaning by means of syntax, lexicon and phonology.
9. An i_____ act is the act of expressing the speaker's intention; it is the act performed in saying something.
10. A c_____ is to commit the speaker himself to some future course of action.
11. An e_____ is to express feelings or attitude towards an existing state.
12. There are four maxims under the cooperative principle: the maxim of q_____, the maxim of quality, the maxim of relation and the maxim of manner.
13. Pragmatics is the study of speakers' intended m_____, that is, how hearers recognize what is meant even when it isn't actually said or written.
14. Discourse d_____ covers all expressions used to refer to earlier or forthcoming segments of the discourse, such as *in the previous/next chapter*.
15. Do not say what you believe to be false—this is the maxim of q_____ that speakers are supposed to follow but also able to flout.
16. Actions performed via utterances are generally called speech acts, and the verbs used to perform actions are called p_____ verbs.
17. Which type of speech act is actually intended by the speaker can be identified by specifying f_____ conditions—circumstances under which it sounds appropriate.

III. Mark the choice that can best complete the statement.

(   ) 1. _____ does not study meaning in isolation, but in context.
   A. Pragmatics   B. Semantics   C. Sense relation   D. Concept

(   ) 2. The meaning of language was considered as something _____ in traditional semantics.
   A. contextual   B. behaviouristic   C. intrinsic   D. logical

(   ) 3. What essentially distinguishes semantics and pragmatics is whether in the study of meaning _____ is considered.
   A. reference   B. speech act   C. practical usage   D. context

(   ) 4. A sentence is a _____ concept, and the meaning of a sentence is often studied in isolation.
   A. pragmatic   B. grammatical   C. mental   D. conceptual

(   ) 5. If we think of a sentence as what people actually utter in the course of communication, it becomes a(n) _____.
   A. constative   B. directive   C. utterance   D. expressive

(   ) 6. Which of the following is true?
   A. Utterances usually do not take the form of sentences.
   B. Some utterances cannot be restored to complete sentences.
   C. No utterances can take the form of sentences.
   D. All utterances can be restored to complete sentences.

(   ) 7. Speech act theory did not come into being until _____.
   A. in the late 50's of the 20th century
   B. in the early 1950's
   C. in the late 1960's
   D. in the early 21st century

(   ) 8. _____ is the act performed by or resulting from saying something; it is the consequence of, or the change brought about by the utterance.
   A. A locutionary act   B. An illocutionary act
   C. A perlocutionary act   D. A performative act

( ) 9. According to Searle, the illocutionary point of the representative is
_____.

A. to get the hearer to do something

B. to commit the speaker to something's being the case

C. to commit the speaker to some future course of action

D. to express the feelings or attitude towards an existing state of affairs

( ) 10. All the acts that belong to the same category share the same purpose, but they differ _____.

A. in their illocutionary acts   B. in their intentions expressed

C. in their strength or force   D. in their effect brought about

( ) 11. _____ is advanced by Paul Grice.

A. Cooperative Principle

B. Politeness Principle

C. The General Principle of Universal Grammar

D. Adjacency Principle

( ) 12. When any of the maxims under the cooperative principle is flouted, _____ might arise.

A. impoliteness   B. contradictions

C. mutual understanding   D. conversational implicatures

IV. Define the following terms.

pragmatics	context	utterance meaning
sentence meaning	constative	performative
locutionary act	illocutionary act	perlocutionary act
cooperative principle	speech act theory	deixis
reference	anaphora	presupposition
indirect speech act	politeness principle	

V. Answer the following questions as comprehensively as possible. Give examples for illustration if necessary.

1. How are semantics and pragmatics different from each other?
2. How does a sentence differ from an utterance?
3. How does a sentence meaning differ from an utterance meaning?
4. Discuss in detail the locutionary act, illocutionary act and perlocutionary act.
5. Searle classified illocutionary act into five categories. Discuss each of them in detail with examples.
6. What are the four maxims under the cooperative principle?
7. How does the flouting of the maxims give rise to conversational implicatures?
8. Analyze the following dialogue with reference to Grice's Cooperative Principle.

   A: I know you are a famous sociologist. Could you define the term "culture", please?

   B: Well, culture is culture. That's it.
9. Please describe two noticeable features of caretaker speech.
10. What are the five general types of illocutionary speech acts John Searle has specified? Give one example to each of them.
11. Illustrate the difference between constative and performative utterance.
12. Explain the relationship between cooperative principle and conversational implicature.
13. When a teacher says "It's so hot in here." during a class, what does she probably mean? Refer to the theory of pragmatics when you analyze the situation.
14. Describe the following exchange in terms of the Speech Act Theory, the Cooperative Principle and the Politeness Principle.

    Carol: Are you coming to the party tonight?

    Lara: I've got an exam tomorrow.
15. Draw out the adjacency pairs in the following conversation.

    Debby: Have you been to Como yet?

    Dan: We went last week.

Debby: How do you get there?

Dan: We went by bus, and returned by hydrofoil.

Debby: Anything to see there?

Dan: Depends what you're interested in.

Debby: I mean, any historical monuments, and maybe some interesting shopping.

Dan: It's got a nice cathedral, and lots of silk.

Debby: I'd like to go on Saturday. Do you want to join me? (Verschueren 1999:39)

16. Analyze the following items with Grice's Cooperative Principle, focus on finding which maxim is flouted in each item.

   (1) He is a tiger.

   (2) Tom has wooden ears.

   (3) If he comes, he comes.

   (4) Girls are girls.

   (5) I'm Alex from Leeds, 26, unmarried.

   (6) A: I'm out of petrol.

      B: There is a garage around the corner.

   (7) A: Shall we get something for the kids?

      B: Yes. But I veto I-C-E-C-R-E-A-M.

   (8) A: I know you are a famous sociologist. Could you define the term "culture", please?

      B: Well, culture is culture. That's it.

17. What does pragmatics study? How does it differ from traditional semantics?

18. How is the notion of context interpreted?

19. How are sentence meaning and utterance meaning related, and how do they differ?

20. Try to think of contexts in which the following sentences can be used for other purposes than just stating facts.

   (1) The room is messy.

   (2) I can't work under untidy circumstances.

(3) It would be good if she had a green skirt on.

21. According to Austin, what are the three acts a person is possibly performing while making an utterance. Give an example.

22. In conversation, speakers may mean exactly what they say and no more. Or they can mean more than what they say, or at an extreme, opposite to what they say. Use examples to illustrate each case. Do you think there are other possibilities?

23. Context is one of the most important factors when we conduct pragmatic analysis. Without the knowledge of the context involved, comprehension is often impossible. Look at the following pictures accompanying a campus news report (here an excerpt) "*a particular Chinese character was 'written'*, 节 *('jie'; to save), ... by 42 light-on and light-off dormitory rooms*". At the end of the report, there is a line "*Use energy-saving lamps*". Which category of speech acts (according to Searle's classification) does this utterance belong to? What are the contextual elements helping you reach the judgement?

24. Language used in public places is generally meant to do things. Look at the following website headers. What are the locutionary act, illocutionary act, and perlocutionary act respectively in each case?

(1)

(2)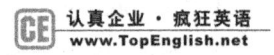

25. How would you describe this short exchange in terms of the Cooperative Principle?

    Carol: Are you coming to the party tonight?

    Lara: I've got an exam tomorrow.

26. Which maxim of the Politeness Principle does this speaker seem to be particularly careful about.

    Well, to be quite honest, I don't think she is ill today.

Chapter 7
Discourse Analysis
话语分析

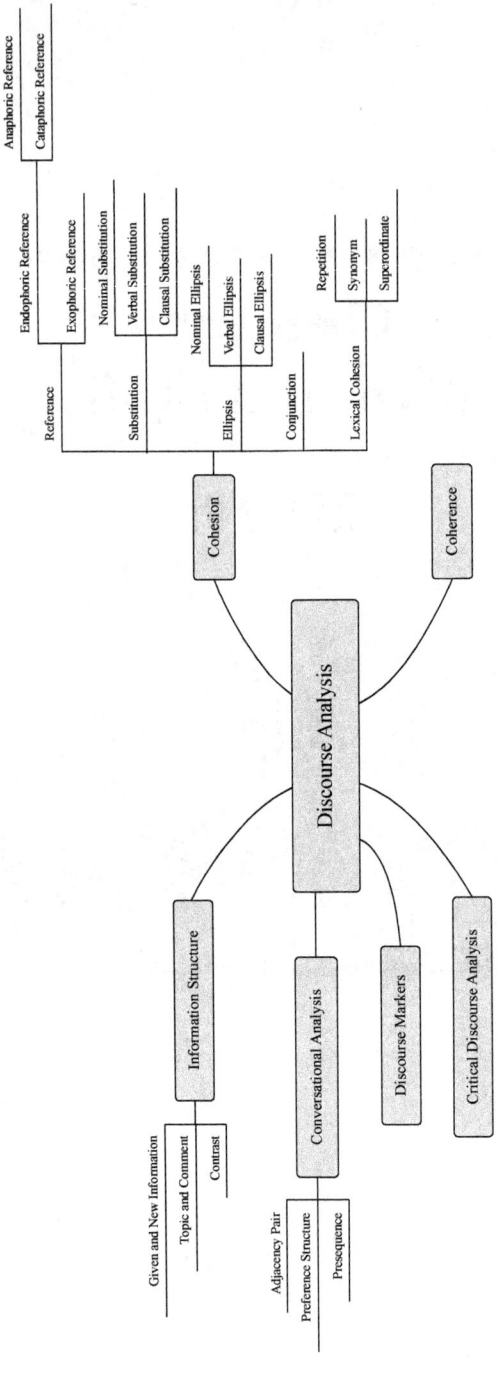

Figure 7 A Mindmap of Discourse Analysis

Chapter 7 Discourse Analysis

> **Key Points**
> Discourse Analysis is the study of how sentences in spoken or written language form larger meaningful units such as paragraphs, conversations, interviews, etc.

I. Decide whether each of the following statements is true or false.

(　) 1. Semantic anomaly is the case that one of the arguments or the predicate of the main prediction is appropriate.

(　) 2. Selectional restrictions are the restrictions on the type of adverbs that can be selected with each verb.

(　) 3. Homonymy is the case that two or more meanings may be associates with the same linguistic form.

(　) 4. Registers are the type of language which is selected as appropriate to a type of situation.

(　) 5. Displacement is the phenomenon that human language can cope with any subject whatever, and it does not matter how far away the topic of conversation is in time and space.

(　) 6. Language interference is the use of elements from one language while speaking another.

(　) 7. Design features are the framework proposed by Hockett, which discusses the defining properties of human language as against snail communication.

(　) 8. Diglossia is a sociolinguistic situation where three varieties of a language exist side by side throughout the community, with each having a definite role to play.

(　) 9. Constituent is any linguistic form or group of linguistic forms that appears at the bottom of one of the lines in the tree diagram of the syntactic analysis.

(　) 10. Complementary distribution is the phenomena that allophones occur in different phonetic environments.

A Collection of Exercises in Linguistics

II. Mark the choice that can best complete the statement.

( ) 1. Of the following, what are the two types of phonetics?
  A. Acoustic and electric.
  B. Arbitrary and auditory.
  C. Articulatory and acoustic.
  D. Allophonic and allomorphic.

( ) 2. "He" and "she" are not examples of gender agreement in English, because _____.
  A. they are pronouns
  B. they need not agree with other words in an English sentence
  C. they mark biological/social gender
  D. both B and C

( ) 3. According to Noam Chomsky, language is the product of _____.
  A. an innate faculty, unique to humans
  B. communication
  C. environmental conditioning
  D. all of the above

( ) 4. The English language has _____.
  A. morphemes
  B. syntax
  C. number agreement
  D. all of the above

( ) 5. Which one of the following statements about errors in foreign language learning is FALSE?
  A. Errors cannot be avoided in foreign language learning.
  B. Errors tell the teacher how far towards the goal the learner has progressed and consequently what remains for him to learn.
  C. Errors are something bad that should not be allowed in foreign language learning.
  D. Errors provide the researcher with evidence of how language is learned or acquired, what strategies or procedures the learner is employing is his discovery of the language.

(　) 6. The use of non-standard English persists because _____.
　　A. the working class is incapable of speaking "correctly"
　　B. English is a complicated and therefore difficult language to master
　　C. subordinate groups use non-standard English to promote solidarity
　　D. teachers do not properly stress the importance of Standard English in schools

(　) 7. Which of the following statements is FALSE?
　　A. Language is just for communication.
　　B. Language is one of many ways in which we experience the world.
　　C. Language is a sign system.
　　D. Language is arbitrary and conventional.

(　) 8. A phoneme is _____.
　　A. the smallest meaningful unit in language
　　B. the smallest unit in language
　　C. the same as an allophone
　　D. both B and C

(　) 9. The Black English sentence "I don't gotta do nothing" is considered incorrect because _____.
　　A. it contains a double negative and is thus inherently incorrect
　　B. it is impossible to understand
　　C. it is not associated with the upper class use of Standard English
　　D. both A and B

III. Define the following terms.

sociolect	bilingualism	utterance meaning
a speech community	performatives	registers
a proposition	an utterance	constatives
the Whorf-Sapir hypothesis		

Chapter 8
Teaching Methodologies and Testing

语言教学与测试

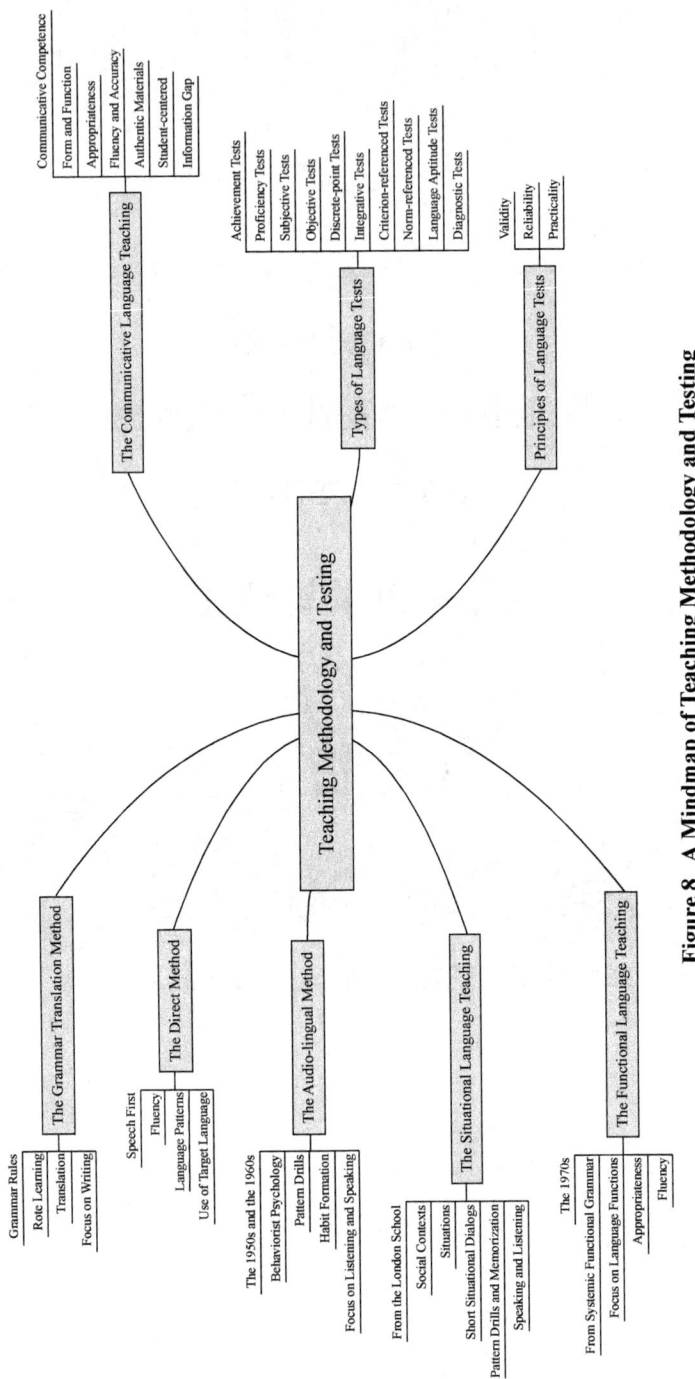

Figure 8 A Mindmap of Teaching Methodology and Testing

Chapter 8　Teaching Methodologies and Testing

> ***Key Points***
>
> Teaching Methodology: the Grammar Translation Method, the Direct Method, the Audio-lingual Method, the Situational Language Teaching, the Functional Language Teaching, the Communicative Language Teaching

I. Mark the choice that can best complete the statement.

(　) 1. "Underlining all the past form verbs in the dialogue" is a typical exercise focusing on _____.

    A. use   B. form   C. meaning   D. function

(　) 2. Which of the following activities may be more appropriate to help students practice a new structure immediately after presentation in class?

    A. Role play   B. Group discussion

    C. Pattern drill   D. Written homework

(　) 3. When teaching students how to give appropriate responses to a congratulation or an apology, the teacher is probably teaching at _____.

    A. lexical level   B. sentence level

    C. grammatical level   D. discourse level

(　) 4. Which of the following activities can help develop the skill of listening for gist?

    A. Listen and find out where Jim lives.

    B. Listen and decide on the best title for the passage.

    C. Listen and underline the words the speaker stresses.

    D. Listen to pairs of words and tell if they are the same.

(　) 5. When an EFL teacher asks his students "How do you know that the author liked the place since he did not tell us explicitly?", he/she is helping students to reach _____ comprehension.

    A. literal   B. appreciative   C. inferential   D. evaluative

( ) 6. Which of the following types of questions are mostly used for checking literal comprehension of the test?
   A. Display questions   B. Rhetorical questions
   C. Evaluation questions   D. Referential questions

( ) 7. Peer-editing during class is an important step of the _____ approach to teaching writing.
   A. genre-based   B. content-based
   C. process-oriented   D. product-oriented

( ) 8. Portfolios, daily reports and speech delivering are typical means of _____.
   A. norm-referenced test   B. criterion-referenced test
   C. summative assessment   D. formative assessment

( ) 9. Which of the following activities can be used to check students' understanding of difficult sentences in the text?
   A. Paraphrasing   B. Blank-filling   C. Story-telling   D. Summarizing

( ) 10. When a teacher organizes group work, which of the following might be of the least concern?
   A. Increasing peer interaction.   B. Increasing individual practice.
   C. Developing language accuracy.   D. Providing variety and dynamics.

( ) 11. If a teacher asks students to collect, compare and analyze certain sentence patterns, he/she aims at developing students' _____.
   A. discourse awareness   B. cultural awareness
   C. strategic competence   D. linguistic competence

( ) 12. When a teacher says to the whole class, *"Stand up and act out the dialogue"*, he/she is playing the role a(an) _____.
   A. monitor   B. organizer   C. assessor   D. prompter

Chapter 8　Teaching Methodologies and Testing

(　) 13. Which of the following may better check students' ability of using a grammatical structure?
A. Having them work out the rule.
B. Having them give some examples.
C. Having them explain the meaning.
D. Having them explain the structure.

(　) 14. The first P in the PPP teaching model stands for _____, which aims to get learners to perceive the form and meaning of a structure.
A. practice　　B. production　　C. presentation　　D. preparation

(　) 15. The main objective of mechanical practice is to help learners to absorb thoroughly the _____ of a language item.
A. meaning　　B. function　　C. context　　D. form

(　) 16. The _____ method is more fitted to the explicit presentation of grammar when the basic structure is being identified.
A. inductive　　B. contrastive　　C. comparative　　D. deductive

(　) 17. Which of the following can be regarded as a communicative language task?
A. Information-gap activity.　　B. Dictation.
C. Sentence transformation.　　D. Blank-filling.

(　) 18. English teachers often ask students to _____ a passage to get the gist of it.
A. skim　　B. scan　　C. predict　　D. describe

(　) 19. In writing, students may not know how to put something into proper English and thus ask their teacher for help. Here the teacher is to play the role of a/an _____.
A. facilitator　　B. assessor　　C. controller　　D. participant

(　) 20. A/An _____ language test, such as IELTS or TOEFL, is developed on the basis of a fixed standard.
A. norm-referenced　　　　B. peer-referenced
C. individual-referenced　　D. criterion-referenced

83

(   ) 21. Which of the following focus(es) on accuracy in teaching grammar?
       A. Simulation B. Substitution drills   C. Role play D. Discussion

(   ) 22. When a teacher says "Next, please pay attention to the time of arrival and departure of the planes in the recording.", he/she intends to develop students' skill of _____ .
       A. predicting   B. getting the general picture
       C. distinguishing sounds   D. getting specific information

(   ) 23. The teacher would use _____ to help students communicate in teaching speaking.
       A. substitution drills   B. group discussion
       C. listening and acting   D. reading aloud

(   ) 24. _____ assessment is used to measure how the performance of a particular students or group of students compares with that of another.
       A. Criterion-referenced   B. Norm-referenced
       C. Formative   D. Summative

(   ) 25. Which of the following teacher's instructions could serve the purpose of eliciting ideas?
       A. Shall we move on?
       B. Read after me, everyone.
       C. What can you see in this picture?
       D. What does the world "quickly" mean?

(   ) 26. Which of the following is an example of teachers' indirect corrective feedback?
       A. Say "went" instead of "go".
       B. We never use "at" that way.
       C. Choice A is not the right answer.
       D. Who can help him with this sentence?

(   ) 27. Total Physical Response as a TEFL method is more often used for teaching _____ .
       A. children   B. adults   C. ES course   D. GE course

Chapter 8 Teaching Methodologies and Testing

( ) 28. Which of the following can NOT be used as a pre-reading task?
   A. Predicting what a passage is about.
   B. Creating a word web related to a topic.
   C. Listening to the recording of a passage.
   D. Sharing what is already known about a topic.

( ) 29. If a teacher gives commands in English and asks students to show understanding by action or gestures, he/she is most probably using _____.
   A. Communicative Approach   B. Audio-lingual Approach
   C. Grammar Translation Method D. Total Physical Response

( ) 30. To assess how well students are able to apply what they have learned in completing a given task, a teacher would use _____ assessment.
   A. performance   B. self   C. competence   D. peer

( ) 31. Popular as it might be, the Presentation-Practice-Production teaching model is not considered appropriate in teaching _____.
   A. phonetics   B. grammar   C. vocabulary   D. reading

( ) 32. Which of the following assumptions about vocabulary learning contradicts the modern language teaching theories?
   A. The best way to learn words is to use them.
   B. The best way to learn vocabulary is via rote-learning.
   C. An English dictionary is an important aid to students.
   D. Learning a word involves learning more than just the word itself.

( ) 33. When a teacher intends to introduce a new grammar item, which of the following strategies can be used to get students to notice it?
   A. Transformation   B. Input enhancement
   C. Expansion   D. Substitution

(   ) 34. If a teacher attempts to implement the top-down model to teach listening, he/she is likely to present _____.
   A. new words after playing the tape
   B. new words before playing the tape
   C. background information after playing the tape
   D. background information before playing the tape

(   ) 35. To grasp the gist of a passage in a quick way, what may a reader focus on?
   A. The transitional paragraphs
   B. The whole passage
   C. The topic sentences
   D. Every sentence in the passage

(   ) 36. When checking students' understanding of a certain language point in class, which of the following utterances is a teacher expected to make?
   A. "Is it okay?"
   B. "Is it clear to you?"
   C. "Are you clear?"
   D. "Is it all right to everyone"?

(   ) 37. Which of the following features is NOT exhibited by the deductive method?
   A. It saves time.
   B. It pays more attention to form.
   C. It teaches grammar in a decontextualized way.
   D. It encourages students to work out the grammatical rules.

II. Answer the following questions.

1. Teaching methods and approaches often reflect the dominant paradigms of how people learn and how to best teach languages. Select any TWO of the following teaching approaches or methods listed below.
   a) Audio Lingual Method

Chapter 8 Teaching Methodologies and Testing

b) Total Physical Response

c) Silent Way

d) Task-based language teaching

e) Form focused instruction

f) Communicative language teaching

g) Content-based instruction

In a clearly written response about the two teaching approaches you have chosen, provide the following:

(1) describe the selected approaches including the principles and goals of the approaches and any teaching or learning theories that are linked to the approaches;

(2) name one or more proponents of the approaches;

(3) discuss any limitations of the approaches in terms of language skill/ability development.

Refer to relevant literature when appropriate to support your response.

2. To promote L2 acquisition, the following methods/approaches have been developed.

a) Audio-lingual Method

b) Direct Method

c) Total Physical Response (TPR)

d) Task-based Language Teaching

e) Content-based Instruction

f) Communicative Language Teaching

Choose any TWO of the methods listed above. For each one selected, (1) describe the typical types of classroom activities often used for learners, (2) explain the learning principles underlying these classroom activities, and (3) discuss advantages of each of the selected methods in terms of learners' language skill development and classroom implications. Refer to relevant literature in your response.

3. Match the ideas/theories in the left column with their sponsors in the right column.

Competence–performance	Saussure
Sapir-Whorf Hypothesis	Halliday
Systemic-functional grammar	Krashen
Langue–Parole	Chomsky
Communicative competence	Sapir
Input Hypothesis	Hymes

Chapter 9
Language Acquisition
语言习得

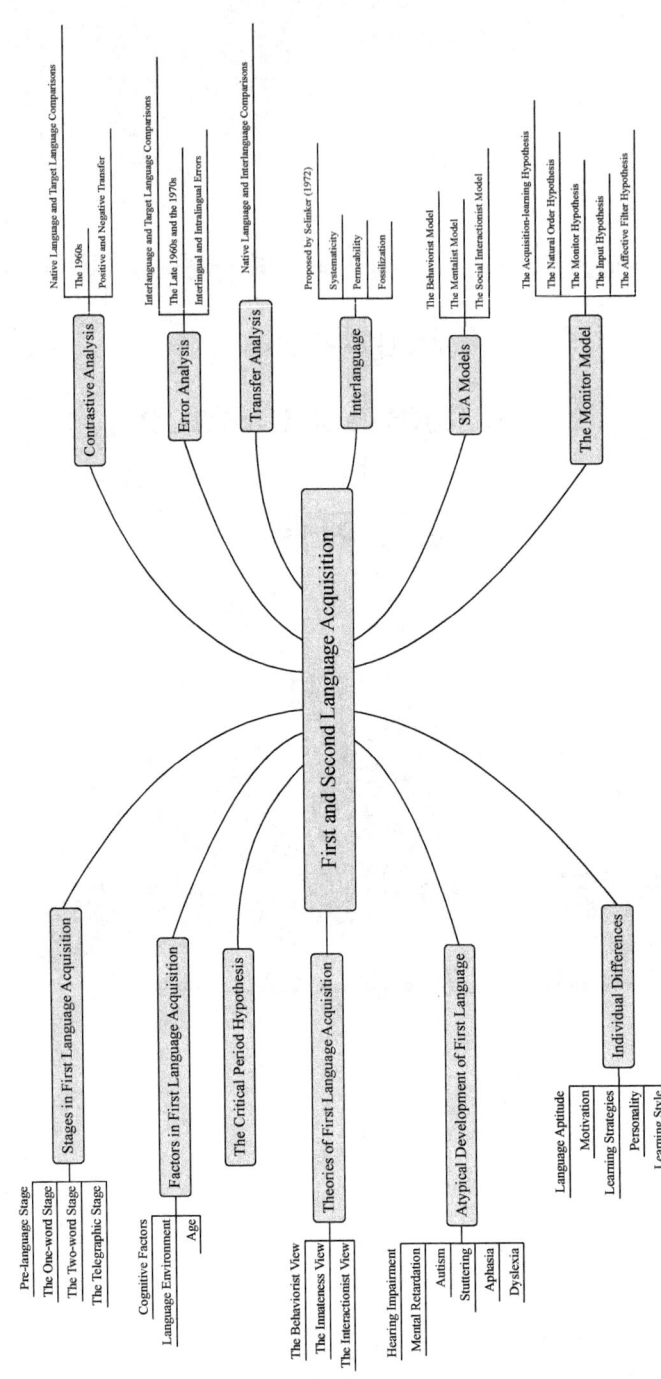

Figure 9 A Mindmap of First and Second Language Acquisition

Chapter 9 Language Acquisition

> **Key Points**
>
> Acquisition is used to refer to picking up a second language through exposure. Learning is used to refer to the conscious study of a second language.

I. Decide whether each of the following statements is true or false.

(　) 1. When children learn to distinguish between the sounds of their language and the sounds that are not part of the language, they can acquire any sounds in their native language once their parents teach them.

(　) 2. The available evidence to date indicates that an explicit teaching of correct forms to young children plays a minor role at best.

(　) 3. Observations of children in different language areas of the world reveal that the developmental stages are similar, possibly universal, whatever the nature of the input.

(　) 4. Significant relationship has been found between talkativeness and overall proficiency in a second language.

(　) 5. The majority of the errors made by the language learners can be explained by mother tongue interference.

(　) 6. Some languages are more challenging to acquire as a first language.

(　) 7. Interlanguage is second language.

(　) 8. Language acquisition is primarily the acquisition of the grammatical system of language.

(　) 9. All normal children have equal ability to acquire their first language.

(　) 10. Children's two-word expressions are absent of syntactic or morphological markers.

(　) 11. Interlanguage is neither the native language nor the second language.

(　) 12. A large proportion of grammatical errors in SLA can be explained by mother tongue interference.

(   ) 13. The capacity to acquire one's first language is a fundamental human trait that all human beings are equally well possessed with.

(   ) 14. Human beings are genetically predetermined to acquire language; this genetic predisposition is a sufficient condition for language development.

(   ) 15. Krashen assumed that there were two independent means or routes of second language learning: acquisition and learning.

(   ) 16. There are two interacting factors in determining language transfer in second language learning.

(   ) 17. Acculturation is a process of adapting to the culture and value system of the second language community.

(   ) 18. The term "learning", when used of language, refers to the gradual development of ability in a language by using it naturally in communicative situation. The term "acquisition", however, applied to a conscious process of accumulating knowledge of vocabulary and grammar of a language.

(   ) 19. In mother tongue acquisition, normal children are not necessarily equally successful.

(   ) 20. Humans can be said to be predisposed and biologically programmed to acquire at least one language.

(   ) 21. Correction and reinforcement are not key factors in child language development as they were claimed to be.

(   ) 22. Language acquisition begins at about the same time as lateralization does and is normally complete, as far as the essentials are concerned, by the time that the process of lateralization comes to an end.

(   ) 23. Input refers to the language which a learner bears and receives and from which he or she can learn.

(   ) 24. Three important characteristics of interlanguage: systemacticity, permeability and fossilization.

(   ) 25. Intrinsic motivation: learners learn a second language for external purposes.

(　) 26. Fossilization, a process that sometimes occurs in language learning in which incorrect linguistic features (such as the accent of a grammatical pattern) become a permanent part of the way a person speaks or writes in the target language.
(　) 27. A second language can only be learned. It can not be acquired.
(　) 28. L1 development and L2 development seem to involve the same processes.
(　) 29. Children first acquire the sounds in all languages of the world, no matter what language they are exposed to, and in late stages acquire the more difficult sounds.
(　) 30. If a child is deprived of linguistic environment, he or she is unlikely to learn a language successfully later on.
(　) 31. Imitation plays at best a very minor role in the child's mastery of language.
(　) 32. Some languages are inferior, or superior, to other languages.
(　) 33. Children who grow up in culture where caretaker speech is absent acquire their native language more slowly than children who are exposed to caretaker speech.
(　) 34. A child's babbling seems to depend on the presence of acoustic, auditory input.
(　) 35. Language acquisition is primarily the acquisition of the vocabulary and the meaning of language.
(　) 36. Conscious knowledge of linguistic rules does ensure acquisition of the rules and therefore an immediate guidance for actual performance.
(　) 37. For the vast majority of children, language development occurs spontaneously and requires little conscious instruction on the part of adults.
(　) 38. In general, the two-word stage begins roughly in the second half of the child's first year.

( ) 39. Children follow a similar acquisition schedule of predictable stages along the route of language development across cultures, though there is an idiosyncratic variation in the amount of time that takes individuals to master different aspects of the grammar.

II. **Fill in each of the following blanks with one word which begins with the letter given.**

1. Learners subconsciously use their first language knowledge in learning a second language. This is known as language t_____.
2. Linguists often use the term native language or mother tongue instead of first language, and t_____ language instead of second language in second language acquisition literature.
3. The language that a learner constructs at a given stage of SLA is known as i_____.
4. Motivation in language learning can be defined in terms of the learner's overall goal or orientation. I_____ motivation occurs when the learner's goal is functional and i_____ motivation occurs when the learner's goal is social.
5. The critical period hypothesis refers to a period in one's life extending from about age two to p_____, during which the human brain is most ready to acquire a particular language and language learning can proceed easily, swiftly and without explicit instruction.
6. A_____ refers to the gradual and subconscious development of ability in the first language by using it naturally in daily communicative situations.
7. The C_____ Analysis was founded on the belief that it was possible, by establishing the linguistic differences between the native and target language systems, to predict what problems learners of a particular second language would face and the types of errors they would make.
8. The first language a_____ refers to the development of a first or native language.

9. According to a n_____ view of language acquisition, humans are equipped with the neural prerequisites for language and language use, just as birds are biologically prewired to learn the songs of their species.

10. A caretaker speech, also called m_____ or b_____, is the type of modified speech typically addressed to young children.

11. B_____ learning theory suggested that a child's verbal behavior was conditioned through association between a stimulus and the following response.

12. Children's one-word utterances are also called h_____ sentences, because they can be used to express a concept or predication that would be associated with an entire sentence in adult speech.

13. In the process of first language acquisition, children usually construct their personal grammars, and their language develops in stages until it a_____ the grammatical rules of the adult language.

14. When a p_____ comes to be adopted by a population as its primary language and children learn it as their first language, it becomes c_____.

15. The early multiword utterances of children lack inflectional morphemes and most minor lexical categories, they are often referred to as t_____ speech.

III. Mark the choice that can best complete the statement.

(　) 1. Which of the following best states the behaviorist view of child language acquisition?
　　A. Language acquisition is a process of habit formation.
　　B. Language acquisition is the species-specific property of human beings.
　　C. Children are born with an innate ability to acquire language.
　　D. Humans are equipped with the neural prerequisites for language and language use.

(   ) 2. Interlanguage is a product of _____.
   A. second language training
   B. mother tongue interference
   C. learning and communicative strategies of the learner
   D. all of the above

(   ) 3. Which of the following is not true?
   A. Interlanguage is a product of communicative strategies of the learner.
   B. Interlanguage is a product of mother tongue interference.
   C. Interlanguage is a product of overgeneralization of the target language rules.
   D. Interlanguage is the representation of learners' unsystematic L2 rules.

(   ) 4. Language acquisition is contrasted with language learning on the ground that acquisition is _____, and focuses on _____.
   A. subconscious, form   B. conscious, form
   C. subconscious, meaning   D. conscious, meaning

(   ) 5. _____ motivation occurs when the learner desires to learn a second language in order to communicate with native speakers of the target language.
   A. Instrumental   B. Functional   C. Integrative   D. Social

(   ) 6. In first language acquisition, imitation plays _____.
   A. a minor role   B. a significant role
   C. a basic role   D. no role

(   ) 7. Language acquisition is primarily the acquisition of the _____ system of language.
   A. phonological   B. semantic   C. grammatical   D. communicative

Chapter 9 Language Acquisition

(　　) 8. Which of the following statements is NOT true of the characteristics at the two-word stage of the first language acquisition?
    A. At first, children's utterances appear to be strings of two holophrastic utterances.
    B. Later they begin to form actual two-word sentences with clear syntactic and semantic relations.
    C. Children's two-word expressions contain some inflectional affixes.
    D. Children's two-word utterances can express a certain variety of grammatical relations indicated by word order.

(　　) 9. A focal point of SLA research has been the nature and development of L2 learners' _____.
    A. second language　　　　　　B. first language
    C. foreign language　　　　　　D. interlanguage

(　　) 10. In a sense, humans can be said to be biologically programmed to acquire at least one language. What is meant by this _____ view of language acquisition is that humans are equipped with the neural prerequisites for language and language use.
    A. behaviorist　B. nativist　　C. mentalist　　　D. empiricist

(　　) 11. Language acquisition device (LAD) came from _____.
    A. John B. Watson　　　　　　B. B. F. Skinner
    C. S. D. Krashen　　　　　　　D. Chomsky

(　　) 12. _____ is one of the main features of interlanguage.
    A. Fossilization　　　　　　　　B. Utilization
    C. Assimilation　　　　　　　　D. Deletion

(　　) 13. Which of the following stages does not belong to the stages of first language acquisition?
    A. The one-word stage　　　　　B. The two-word stage
    C. The three-word stage　　　　D. None of the above

( ) 14. According to Krashen, _____ refers to the gradual and subconscious development of ability in the first language by using it naturally in daily communicative situations.
    A. learning   B. competence   C. performance   D. acquisition

( ) 15. A distinction was made between _____ and _____. The former would facilitate target language learning, the later would interfere it.
    A. positive transfer, negative transfer
    B. negative transfer, positive transfer
    C. contrastive analysis, error analysis
    D. error analysis, contrastive analysis

( ) 16. Linguists have found that for the vast majority of children, language development occurs _____.
    A. with much imitation
    B. with little conscious instruction
    C. with much correction from their parents
    D. with little linguistic input

( ) 17. According to the _____, the acquisition of a second language involves, and is dependent on, the acquisition of the culture of the target language community.
    A. acculturation view   B. mentalist view
    C. behaviorist view   D. conceptualist view

( ) 18. In general, a good second learner is an adolescent _____.
    A. who has a strong and well-defined motivation to learn
    B. who seeks out all chances to interact with the input
    C. who is willing to identify himself with the culture of the target language community
    D. all of the above

( ) 19. The formal instruction in second language acquisition _____.
    A. has no effect at all   B. has a powerful delayed effect
    C. has very little effect   D. has unsatisfactory effect

( ) 20. _____ is believed to be a major source of incorrect forms resistant to further instruction.
A. The second language learners' unwillingness to learn
B. The Poor classroom teaching
C. The fossilization of the learner's interlanguage
D. The learner's lack of instrumental motivation

( ) 21. _____, except those with mental or physical impairments, are better or worse first language acquirers.
A. Some men   B. Almost all men   C. No men   D. Few men

( ) 22. In first language acquisition children usually _____ grammatical rules from the linguistic information they hear.
A. use   B. accept   C. generalize   D. reconstruct

( ) 23. Basically all the following categories except _____ are always missing in the children's telegraphic speech stage.
A. the copula verb "be"   B. inflectional morphemes
C. function words   D. content words

( ) 24. Generally speaking, _____ is not the theories concerning how language is learned.
A. behaviorist view of language acquisition
B. innatist view of language acquisition
C. interactionist view of language acquisition
D. psychological view of language acquisition

( ) 25. The development of linguistic skills involves the acquisition of _____ rules rather than the mere memorization of words and sentences.
A. cultural   B. grammatical   C. behavior   D. pragmatic

( ) 26. _____ has been found to occur usually in children's pronunciation or reporting of the truthfulness of utterances, rather than in the grammaticality of sentences.
A. Punishment   B. Instruction   C. Reinforcement   D. Imitation

(　) 27. _____ are learners' conscious, goal-oriented and problem-solving based efforts to achieve desirable learning efficiency.
   A. Learning strategies   B. Cognitive strategies
   C. Metacognitive strategies   D. Affect strategies

(　) 28. The optimum age for second language acquisition is _____.
   A. early teenage   B. after puberty
   C. at puberty   D. after the brain lateralization

(　) 29. Writing is a secondary language form based upon _____.
   A. speech   B. gesture   C. emotion   D. sounds

IV. Define the following terms.

acquisition & learning	incidental learning	intentional learning
language	error analysis	interlanguage
Monitor Model	affective filter hypothesis	Universal Grammar
fossilization	Shumann's Acculturation Model	

V. Answer the following questions briefly.

1. Summarize the individual differences in second language acquisition.
2. What are the differences of error analysis from contrastive analysis?
3. What are the beneficial views obtained from the studies on children's L1 acquisition?
4. Discuss the contrastive analysis in detail.
5. What role does UG play in SLA?
6. What are classifications of communication strategies?
7. What is the Critical Period Hypothesis? What are your ideas about it?
8. For behaviorists, L1 acquisition is equal to L2 acquisition. To what extent is second language learning similar to first language learning? Are there any differences between them?

9. What are the components of the monitor model put forward by Krashen?
10. What are the major stages that a child has to follow in first language development? What are the features of the linguistic forms at each stage?
11. What is the role of input for SLA?
12. What are the individual learner factors for SLA?
13. What are learning strategies? Give examples.
14. How do you understand interlanguage?
15. What is the role of correction and reinforcement in first language acquisition?
16. Why do we say language acquisition is primarily the acquisition of the grammatical system of language?
17. Of all the theories you have learned on language acquisition, which one seems to you most reasonable? Why?
18. What's the difference between acquisition and learning according to Krashen?
19. How do the learner factors potentially influence the way in which a second language is acquired?
20. What are the factors influencing the success of SLA?
21. What benefits might accrue to NNSs interacting with one another that they wouldn't necessarily get by conversing with NSs?
22. What are the differences between the Behaviorist learning model and that of Mentalist?
23. What are the main stages of first language acquisition?
24. What features of language do you think should be included in a good, comprehensive definition of language?
25. Discuss the biological basis of language acquisition.
26. What is the role of imitation in first language acquisition?
27. Enumerate some causes that lead to the systematic occurrence of errors in second language acquisition.
28. How does Hatch's view that language learning evolves out of learning how to carry on conversations differ from the traditional sequence in the language classroom?

VI. Fulfill the following tasks.

1. Define and give some examples of communicative strategies.
2. Can caretaker speech and/or FTD affect your views as to the degree to which learning a first or second language is determined by an innate (language) learning capacity? Why or why not?
3. List some features of the speech input to children learning their L1.
4. What is meant by the following terms: "linguistic" "conversational" "interactional" and "elaborative" modification? Give an example of each.
5. If you were interested in researching each of the following questions, which research methodology would you use and why?
   (1) Are there male/female differences in how invitations are extended between native speakers? How does non-native speaker behavior compare?
   (2) Is there a sequence in which the second language pronouns are acquired? If so, what is it?
   (3) Does practice with sentence-combining exercises result in learners producing longer T-units in their classroom composition?
   (4) What are word-attack skills learners naturally use when they encounter a word which they don't know?
   (5) What is the relationship between the age at which second language instruction began and the level of second language proficiency achieved after three years of instruction?
6. Choose a structure which occurs fairly frequently in the second language. Collect some naturalistic data and some data through elicited imitation. How do the two types of data compare?
7. If true, what implications do you think the non-interface and interface positions, respectively would have for materials design and classroom, methodology? What might "consciousness-raising" activities look like, and how might they differ from traditional grammar exercises?

Chapter 9 Language Acquisition

8. How would you operationalize "formal instruction" in a study designed to assess the effect of instruction on IL development? What features might you monitor, and how, in order to determine whether "instruction" had been delivered?

9. Many of the differences observed between speech to foreigners and other NSs concern the relative frequently of certain linguistic items or the relative simplicity/complexity by comparing two (or more) speech corpora. The NS baseline data must be comparable, however. Not any speech will do. What factors make corpora comparable? What factors must you control for, in other words, when collecting data? Can you think of any claims made about differences between FT and speech to/conversation with other NSs that may be due to the use of non-comparable baseline data?

10. Tape yourself or a friend teaching an SL class and also talking informally to one of the non-native students from the same class outside the classroom. Transcribe the two tapes. What similarities and differences do you notice between FT and SL teacher talk? What relevance might the similarities and especially the differences have for the success/failure of language teaching and/or for naturalistic (uninstructed) SLA?

11. If you have the opportunity to study a second language, try keeping a diary on your experience. Record on a regular basis how you feel about the progress you are making: what is helping and what is hindering you in learning the SL. Later, you may choose to sift through the diary entries, looking for particular patterns or salient experiences. See what these reveal about you're an social-psychological, personality, cognitive style, etc. , profile.

12. Which (if any) of the five examples of potential "laws" of SL do you think actually merit the status of hypotheses, generalizations or laws, and why? What other findings of SLA research do you consider strong enough and widely enough attested to merit the status of generalization or law? Would ascription of the status of generalization or law be easier if you recast any of the statements in probabilistic form?

13. The following is an "Accent Inventory" devised by Clifford Prator and Betty Wallace Rabinett in their book *American English Pronunciation*. In the diagnostic passage, all of the phonemes and many of the intonation patterns of English are contained. Read it over and make a list of predictions about where you think a speaker of a particular native language with which you are familiar is likely to have difficulty. Next, tape a native speaker of the particular language as he or she reads the diagnostic passage. Listen to the tape to determine how many of your predictions were confirmed. Were there other errors that were made that you had not anticipated? What other observations can you make?

Diagnostic passage

(1) When a student from another country comes to study in the United States, he has to find the answers to many questions, and he has many problems to think about.

(2) Where should he live?

(3) Would it be better if he looked for a private room off campus or if he stayed in a dormitory?

(4) Should he spend all of his time just studying?

(5) Shouldn't he try to take advantage of the many social and cultural activities which are offered?

(6) At first it is not easy for him to be casual in dress, informal in manner, and confident in speech.

(7) Little by little he learns what kind of clothing is usually wore here to be casually dressed for classes.

(8) He also learns to choose the language and customs which are appropriate for informal situations.

(9) Finally, he begins to feel sure of himself.

(10) But let me tell you, my friend, this long-awaited feeling doesn't develop suddenly, does it?

(11) All of this takes practice.

14. In light of what is known about cross-linguistic influence, what differences (if any) do you think desirable between language teaching materials for use with classes of learners with the same L1 and those for use with learners with a variety of different L1s? Are "English for Japanese speakers" or "French for speakers of German" meaningful titles for textbooks?
15. What other examples of implicational markedness relationships might show the same "domino" effect for instruction as the relative-clause studies, whereby instruction is a more marked construction generalizes to less marled ones? Design a study to test your ideas.
16. Why might interlanguage variability and systematicity be relevant for teachers when giving feedback on learners' errors? What practical ways can you suggest for teachers to asses these dimensions of their students' interlanguages?

Chapter 10
Cognitive Linguistics
认知语言学

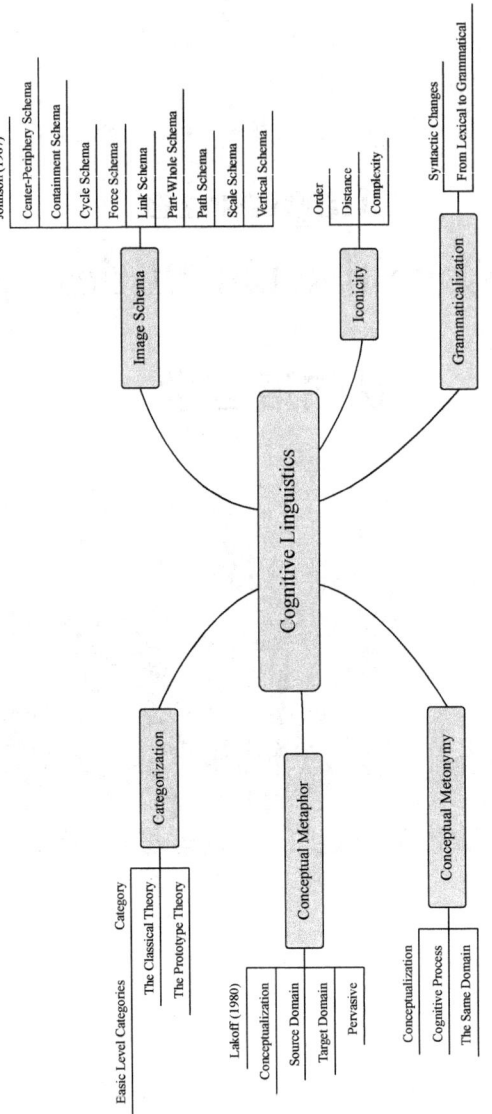

Figure 10　A Mindmap of Cognitive Linguistics

Chapter 10 Cognitive Linguistics

> **Key Points**
> Cognitive Linguistics is the study of language and the mind rather than a single articulated theoretical framework.

Ⅰ. **Decide whether each of the following statements is true or false.**

(   ) 1. Language is always necessary for the functioning of thought because thinking can't take place without language.

(   ) 2. Basic level categories are the categories of words which are most commonly used.

(   ) 3. Cognitive linguistics is a new branch of linguistics within the framework of second generation cognitive science.

Ⅱ. **Define the following terms.**

cognitive linguistics	cognitive grammar	cognitive semantics
prototype	grammaticalization	conceptual metaphor
categorization	iconicity	blending theory
construction grammar	family resemblance	conceptual metaphor theory

Ⅲ. **Fulfill the following tasks.**

1. First read the following monologue and try to establish what and whom the speaker is talking about. Then give an analysis of the referential coherence in the text by answering the questions below.

   a) Well, a friend called me;
   b) a friend of hers who I know,
   c) last week she called
   d) and said: "Well, you have company.
   e) Jan fell down four flight of steps."

f) They have a house like this,

g) and she was going to a luncheon

h) and the women were honking the horn outside.

i) She heard them, right?

j) And usually she lets the door open

k) But she didn't this time.

l) So she comes running down the steps

m) and she fell down four

n) and landed on her side.

o) Her right side's fractured.

(1) First underline all the referential expressions (pronouns and full noun phrases) in the text.

(2) Identify each referential expression as presenting new information (N) or as presenting information that has already been introduced (given information: G).

(3) Identify each referential expressions as presenting exophoric (EX) reference or as presenting endophoric reference (EN).

(4) Classify the given endophoric elements as cataphoric (C) or anaphoric (A). As you saw in this chapter, endophoric elements may be conceptually prominent (and realized by a pronoun or ellipted) or non-prominent (usually realized by full noun-phrases). In this text, however, this correlation between prominence and linguistic form is clearly broken by the use of "they" in (f). Explain how the hearer is able to make sense of this form.

2. In what way are the following expressions iconic? (sequential order, distance, quantity)

(1) The Krio word for "earthquake" is shaky-shaky.

(2) Department store ad: We have rails and rails and rails of famous fashion.

(3) Police warning: Don't drink and drive!

(4) Japanese ie "house", ieie "houses"

(5) See Naples and die.

(6) I swear by Almighty God that what I am about to say is the truth, the whole truth, and nothing but the truth.
3. The expressions in italics are peripheral members of their particular grammatical category such as noun, adjective, adverb, etc. Why?
   (1) The *approach* has to be simple and low cost.
   (2) This is the *very* man.
   (3) the *then* president
4. Draw up a radial network for the different senses of *paper*.
   (1) The letter was written on good quality paper.
   (2) I need this quotation on paper.
   (3) The police officer asked to see my car papers.
   (4) The examination consisted of two-hour papers.
   (5) The professor is due to give his paper at 4 o'clock.
   (6) Seat sales are down, so we'll have to paper the house this afternoon (Theatrical slang: "to give away free tickets to fill the auditorium").
5. In what way do the indexical principles, egocentricity and anthropocentricity, play a role in the ordering of the following irreversible pairs of words?
   (1) come and go, this and that, here and there
   (2) women and wine, king and country, people and places
   (3) man and beast, man and dog
   (4) friend or foe, win or lose, live or die
6. List basic color terms in English (or your native language) by checking which color terms consist of only one short words and are freely applicable to different kinds of objects and organisms. Describe the color of sweaters, T-shirts, etc., using basic color terms as points of references.
7. For the notion of footwear think of or find as many words as you can, including such terms as boots, slippers, trainers, pumps, flipflops, mountain boots, shoes, wellingtons and add terms such as indoor footwear, sportswear, etc.
   (1) Which of these words are superordinate terms, and which ones subordinate terms?

(2) Which of these words could be considered "basic level terms?" Give reasons for your answer.

(3) Which of these words are highly entrenched, and which ones aren't? Give reasons for your answer.

8. Ask your friends to list attributes for the following words:

table, beds, lamps

knife, fork, spoon

ring, bracelet, necklace

furniture; cutlery; jewellery

Test whether your lists support Rosch's findings about the attribute inventories of basic level categories and superordinates.

9. Arrange the items below in one of the six categories: (a) simple words, (b) compounds, (c) derivations, (d) complex types, (e) syntactic groups and (f) others.

drilling rig   submarine   baptism of fire   spacecraft

water cannon   artificial light   synthetic fibre   the take-away restaurant

10. Consider the following collocations with "strong" and "weak":

a strong drink   strong beer   a strong man   a strong scent   a strong anesthetic

a weak heart   a weak point   weak eye-sight   a weak dose   a weak stomach

a weak man

Is it possible to see these uses as members of prototype categories for STRONG and WEAK? Or should they all be derived from a single dimension, for example "strength" or "intensity", which represents a basic experience?

11. Analyze the following utterances. After identifying them as (i) constitutive, (ii) obligative or (iii) informative speech acts, identify the subtype: (i) a declarative or expressive, (ii) offer or directive, or (iii) assertive or information question. Then, finally, for obligative speech acts decide whether they are direct or indirect.

(1) Shall I get you some coffee?

(2) I hereby declare the meeting closed.

(3) (In a book shop): Where is the linguistics department, please?

(4) (In a Bed and Breakfast): Are you ready for coffee now?

(5) Oh, Jesus, there he goes again.

(6) What the hell are you doing in my room?

(7) Can't you make a little less noise?

12. Look up definitions of emotion terms like anger, rage, hate, disgust, fear, panic, love, affection in several dictionaries and decide whether they are helpful as descriptions of these emotions. Do these definitions make use of metonymies and metaphors?

13. Here are the names of the inhabitants of fourteen European countries.

Austrian	Finn	Norwegian
Belgian	Frenchman	Portuguese
Briton	German	Spaniard
Dane	Irishman	Swede
Dutchman	Italian	

(1) Can you describe the compounding or derivational processes used in the labelling of inhabitants?

(2) Can you find out after what type of word man is used, after what word forms -ian and -ese are used, and in which cases we find conversion?

14. Examine the following emotion categories: PRIDE, ADMIRATION, GRATITUDE, PITY, EMBARRASSMENT, SHAME, GUILT. Can you see a close relationship between these categories and any of the basic emotion categories? Find reasons why they are less basic.

15. The underlined segments in the following words represent different pronunciations. Group the segments accordingly and find the appropriate terms to characterize the differences.

thin–then–mother–cloth–clothes

sees–seize–cease–seizes–ceases–house–houses

16. Compare the written forms and the pronunciations of the following words:

a) horse–worse

b) heart–heard–beard

c) lumber–plumber

d) tough–bough–dough–hiccough

e) broom–brook–brooch

f) tomb–bomb–womb

g) roll–doll

h) golf–wolf

i) seize–sieve

j) kind–kindle

(1) Say whether they rhyme or not

(2) Write the words in phonemic transcription

17. Look at the following compounds containing the element *shoe* and decide in each case which of the source categories is dominant in the categorization of the compound:

ballot shoe

shoe hammer

shoe-shop

canvas shoe

shoe heel

shoe-tip

patent-leather shoe

shoe leather

shoemaker

peep-toe shoe

shoe-boy

sling-back shoe

town shoe

walking shoe

Do any of these compounds suggest attributes that can be derived from neither of the source categories?

18. In the following examples "thanks" is said for different reasons and in different situations. Comment on (i) what the reason or occasion is for the thanks, (ii)

whether it is a formal or informal situation, and (iii) whether the way it is said is appropriate or not for the situation?

    a) "Many thanks for your presents."

    b) Margaret handed him the butter. "Thank you", Samuel said, "Thank you very much."

    c) —"Can I give you a lift to town?", —"Oh, thank you."

    d) —"How was your trip to Paris?", —"Very pleasant, thank you."

    e) The president expressed deep gratitude for Mr. Christopher's service as State Secretary.

19. Check in some older dictionaries whether the words in italics in the following sentences are present already and whether they have their present-day meanings. What can you conclude from this?

    (1) He is a real *anorak*. ("boring person")

    (2) This machinery has highly *sophisticated* equipment. ("clearly designed, advanced")

    (3) This teacher knows how to keep the children on their *toes*. ("alert")

20. What types of sign (iconic, indexical, symbolic) are involved in the following cases?

    (1) inverted triangle as a road sign

    (2) sign depicting falling rocks

    (3) morse signs

    (4) frozen window panes of a car

    (5) speedometer in car

    (6) Burglar alarm going off

    (7) Baby crying

    (8) Dog wagging its tail

    (9) animal drawings in cave dwellings

    (10) A wedding ring

    (11) a clenched fist in the air

    (12) a ring in the nose (human)

21. Here are the definitions for anger, love and hate from the Longman Dictionary of Contemporary English. Are these common words defined in an obscure and/or circular fashion? Can you suggest how the definitions can be re-phrased more clearly?

    anger: A strong feeling of wanting to harm, hurt or criticize someone because they have done something unfair, cruel, offensive etc.

    love: ① Strong feeling of caring about someone, especially a member of your family or a close friend;

    ② A strong feeling of liking and caring about someone, especially combined with sexual attraction.

    hate: An angry unpleasant feeling that someone has when they hate someone and want to harm them.

22. Compare the plural forms of the Proto-West-Germanic words mus and kuh in English,

    German and Dutch and say what similar or different processes took place in each language.

    a. West Germanic: mus–musi   kuh–kuhi
    b. English: mouse–mice   cow OE kine/NE cows
    c. German: Maus–Mouse   Kuh–Kuhe
    d. Dutch: muffs–muizen   koe–koeien

23. Consider the following sentences.

    (1) The haystack was important because the cloth ripped.

    (2) The journey was not delayed because the bottle shattered.

    Does each of these sentences become more meaningful to you if you place it within one of the following frames?

24. Discuss whether in your opinion the notion of cognitive economy is only important for everyday categorization (or folk taxonomies) as opposed to scientific classifications and information processing in computers.

25. In some places it is possible to get "breakfast" at any hour of the day or night. What aspect of our eating habits does this usage depend on? (To put the question another way, how would our eating habits have to be different for the notion "breakfast at any time" to be meaningless?)

26. Select typical examples of the categories NEWSPAPER, JOURNAL, MAGZINE and PERIODICAL. Do you know publications which illustrate the fuzziness of the boundaries between these neighboring categories?

27. Draw pictures of prototypical examples and of objects on the borderline between the categories BOTTLE, GLASS, VASE and BOWL, and use them as stimuli for a naming task with your friends or family.

28. As we found, the vagueness of objects and the fuzziness of categories must be kept apart. Look at the following examples and discuss which of them involve fuzziness or vagueness or both aspects:

mountain	hill	summit	plateau	valley		
hedge	bush	forest	park			
street	road	avenue	drive	highway		
tree	shrub	flower				
river	stream	brook	torrent	firth	estuary	spring

29. The following are all compounds with a color term. Using the notions of specialization, generalization, metaphor and metonymy, say which process applies in each example and try to explain how they are motivated.

bluebell	redroot	black-eyed pea
bluebird	redbreast	blackbird
blue baby	redneck	Black (person)
blueprint	red carpet	black art

30. Collect attributes for the following categories and try to distinguish between objective properties and subjective associations.

| man | woman | boy | girl |
| mansion | palace | cottage | castle |

bicycle	motorbike	car	van	lorry
jeans	leggings	tuxedo	tailcoat	miniskirt

31. Discuss the attribute "fun", "no purpose other than the game itself", "uncertain outcome" and "governed by rules" as candidates for the status of category-wide attributes for the category GAME. Try to come up with other possibilities and discuss possible counterexamples.

32. In pragmatics and sociolinguistics the participants of a speech event are often seen as part of the wider "situational context". Discuss this notion of "context" in relation to the one put forward in this chapter.

33. In Tzeltal plant and animal classification PINE, WILLOW, CORN and GOPHER represent the basic or generic level. Is this also true for your dialect of English or your native language (if this is not English)?

34. In what kind of situation might one utter (1) below and how might this differ from the situation in which one would say (2)?

    (1) I can see the ground.

    (2) I can see (the) land.

35. Find the salient general attribute which is highlighted by the superordinate categories WEAPON, BUILDING, JEWELLERY, TOOL, FOOD, STATIONERY, CLOTHES. Which dimensions are involved?

36. The notion of "parasitic categorization" is based on the view that superordinate categories "borrow" attributes from basic level categories. Alternatively, one might say that basic level categories supply the attributes which are then "transferred" to the respective superordinate categories. Which view do you find more convincing?

37. Compile a list of English prepositions from a grammar book and discuss why some of them seem to be more basic than others.

38. Collect animal metaphors like "He is a real pig" or "She is a bitch" from a dictionary and explain them with the notions "source" and "target model".

39. Use schema theory to explain the little girl's utterance in the following situation.

    Situation:

Chapter 10 Cognitive Linguistics

A family gathering, including a 3-year-old little girl, her parents and grandparents. The adults were talking about various illness a child may have these days. When the grandpa mentioned that one of the girl's kindergarten classmates was ill for he was over fat, the child burst out suddenly:

Utterance:

"He has no illness at all. He never coughs!"

Chapter 11
Language and Culture
语言与文化

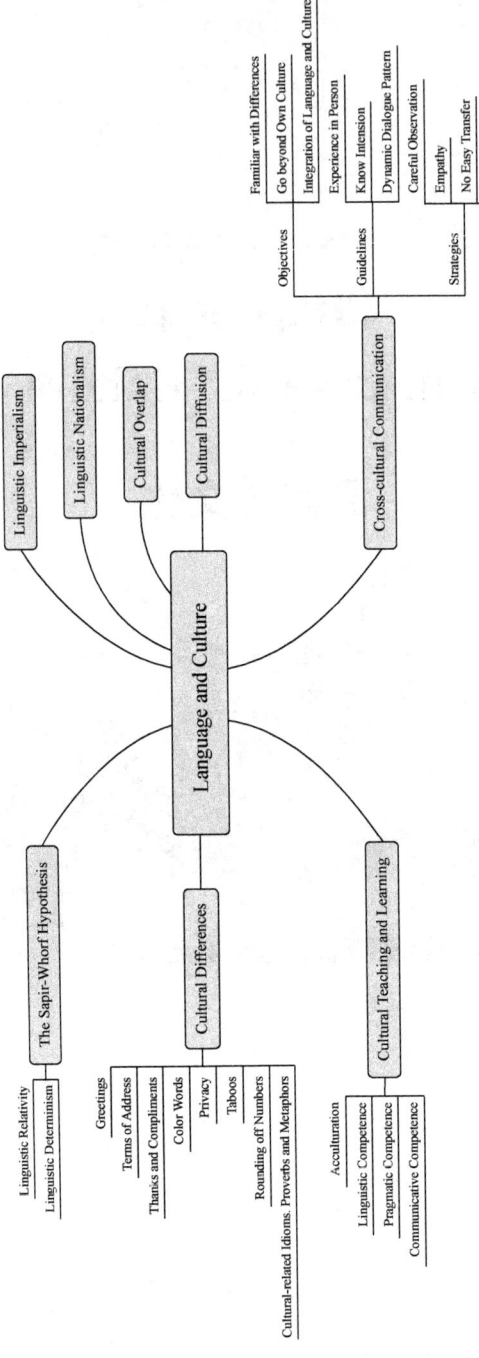

Figure 11 A Mindmap of Language and Culture

Chapter 11 Language and Culture

> **Key Points**
> The relationship between language and culture: Language is part of culture; Language is the carrier and container of culture; Language is influenced and shaped by culture; Language also exerts its influence on culture.

I. Decide whether each of the following statements is true or false.

( ) 1. When we compare culture to an iceberg, we say most of components of culture are hidden under the water.

( ) 2. The fact that successful translation between languages can be made is one of the major arguments against the Sapir-Whorf hypothesis.

( ) 3. Generally speaking, the Americans' postures are more casual than Chinese speakers.

( ) 4. North Americans feel more comfortable when communicating at greater distances. So it is often referred to as noncontact culture.

( ) 5. A well-fitted white suit is appropriate for almost all formal business situations and most social occasions.

( ) 6. In English, people's age, income, political, marital status, and religious beliefs, etc. are normally considered too personal to talk about.

( ) 7. Euphemisms are also frequently used in mass media about political, socioeconomic affairs and international relations to avoid unpleasantness of some terms or expressions.

( ) 8. Chinese greetings and responses are rather formal, and they are normally fixed expressions.

( ) 9. American people take actions very seriously and emphasize their goals. When they accomplish achievements, the outcome is usually measured qualitatively.

( ) 10. Surnames can be used together in addressing Western people after the titles such as doctor, Father, Queen, general, and captain.

(   ) 11. Taboo is a phenomenon unique in Chinese and American cultures.
(   ) 12. In Western culture, visiting others unexpectedly is a taboo.
(   ) 13. Compared with spoken English, written English tends to use longer words of Latin origin, and often relies on rhetorical devices for effectiveness.
(   ) 14. Language by no means determines the ways we perceive the objective world, but by its convenience, availability, and habitual use, does influence the perceptions of human being.
(   ) 15. In American culture, people may send expensive gifts to friends and colleagues in order to show their intimacy or respect.
(   ) 16. In many instances contradictory values are found in a particular culture. That is, there is often a gulf between the values that are articulated (idealism) and the values that are acted out (reality).
(   ) 17. Values people hold exert a strong influence on people's daily life by teaching people how to behave properly.
(   ) 18. In Western culture, people sometimes send 10 flowers to friends or lovers to mean "perfection".
(   ) 19. Conceptual meaning is the core of the meaning of a word. It is relatively constant and stable, because it is the meaning agreed upon by all the members of the same speech community.
(   ) 20. It has been said that there are more than 1000 surnames adopted by English speakers, who currently have 35,000 or so given names available.
(   ) 21. In American English, a number of irregular verbs have become regularized, while remaining irregular in English.
(   ) 22. When describing students, teachers or educators in English speaking countries tend to use positive expressions rather than negative ones in order to avoid hurting the students' and their parents' feeling.
(   ) 23. In a broad sense, culture means the total way of life of a people, including the patterns of belief, customs, objects, institutions, techniques, and language that characterizes the life of the human community.

Chapter 11 Language and Culture

(　) 24. Western people are mainly future-oriented so that they are good at making plans for the future and are likely to ignore their history.

(　) 25. An informal way of addressing the father in a family can be "Father!".

(　) 26. Proverbs are implied or indirect references to characters or events from culture: literature, legends, history, religion, sports, etc.

(　) 27. In English culture, emotional bodily contacts such as kissing, shoulder clapping, hugging are acceptable whether the person you face is a stranger or an acquaintance.

(　) 28. The value that every person desires to live a happy life is typically a universal value rather than an individual value.

(　) 29. In China, the given name is usually used in addressing a person younger in age or lower in rank or used to show intimacy between peers.

(　) 30. Connotative meanings, social meanings and affective meanings can be grouped together as associative meanings.

(　) 31. As guests, American people often repeat their intention of leaving at least twice and do so an hour before his real leaving.

(　) 32. In recent years, the trend of many English-speaking people has been to address others by using the Surname after Mr. or Ms. in order to show their respect.

(　) 33. The standard language is the language used in government and courts of law, and for official business.

(　) 34. In China, talking about certain parts of body or sex is considered improper and obscene.

(　) 35. The example of Eskimo tribes' word use of snow is to illustrate that language also exerts its influence on culture.

(　) 36. In most cultures, presenting a card with two hands convey respect and an appreciation of the importance of the ritual.

(　) 37. In much of Asia, pointing others with the index finger is often considered rude.

( ) 38. Japanese people prefer to speak loudly because loudness for them connotes strength and sincerity.

( ) 39. In China adults are often seen to fondle other people's babies and very small children to show their affection and friendliness.

II. Fill in each of the following blanks with one word which begins with the letter given.

1. In many societies of the world, we find a large number of people who speak more than one language. As a characteristic of societies, b_____ inevitably results from the coming into contact of people with different cultures and different languages.

2. The notion of linguistic determinism and linguistic relativism is called the S_____ hypothesis.

3. The Sapir-Whorf hypothesis includes the notion of linguistic d_____ and linguistic relativism.

4. A_____ is a process of adapting to the culture and value system of the second language community.

5. A s_____ community is one group, all of whose members share the same language or at least a single language variety.

6. Because languages differ in many ways, Whorf also believed that speakers of different languages perceive and experience the world differently, i.e. relative to their linguistic background, thus the notion of linguistic r_____.

7. A related issue with integrative motivation has been the extent to which learners differ in the process of adapting to the new culture of the L2 community. This adaptation process is called a_____.

III. Fill in the blanks.

1. Language and culture, intrinsically interdependent on each other, have _____ together through history.

2. Culture differences are also evident in the way _____ and compliments are expressed.

Chapter 11　Language and Culture

3. Language as the _____ of culture is tightly intertwined with culture.
4. The euphemism of garbage collector is _____.
5. Sometimes English people will tell a white _____, when they feel it is merely more convenient or polite than telling the truth.
6. "Strategic villages or hamlets" is the euphemism for "_____".
7. There are four categories of distance: _____ distance, _____ distance, _____ distance and _____ distance.
8. Chinese people are usually encouraged to be good by the people around them and are likely to feel ashamed if they fail to live up to others' expectations that they should be virtuous. In this case, Chinese culture is called a kind of _____.
9. Social meaning is what a piece of language conveys about the social circumstances of its use, such as the _____, _____, and _____.
10. When it comes to the relationship of human to nature, Chinese culture emphasizes that humans are a part of nature and they should live in _____ with nature.
11. Being subject to instinct, capable of speech, experienced in cookery, skirt or dress wearing, gentle, compassionate, sensitive, and hard-working… are all about the _____ meaning of the word "woman".
12. According to the present Western value of human nature, men are basically a mixture of _____.
13. In Chinese culture, people's behaviors should be suitable to their _____ and characters.
14. Quite a lot Westerners hold such a belief that Chinese people often make their talk with others a performance to show off themselves and their conversation is often lacking in _____.
15. When Liu Ying runs into a British woman on the bus, she'd better immediately say, "_____".
16. It is _____ to greet your foreign teacher John Smith "Professor John!".
17. "Every man is the architect for his own fortune." vividly indicates American value of _____.

A Collection of Exercises in Linguistics

18. _____ and _____ are the typical two features of Chinese features of collectivism.
19. Language is a system of _____ _____ symbols used for human communication.
20. _____ are pleasant, polite or harmless sounding words or expressions used to mask harsh, rude or infamous truths.
21. Culture reflects a total way of life of a people in a _____.
22. In a word, _____ expresses culture reality.
23. Culture has the properties of being _____, _____, _____, _____, and _____.
24. There may be some nonverbal ways of greeting such as _____ and _____.
25. When Li Ming's American friend Leo came to visit his house, if Li Ming's mother wants to offer some tea, it's appropriate for her to ask Leo, _____?

IV. Mark the choice that can best complete the statement.

( ) 1. What's the meaning of "a lucky dog" in English?
    A. a clever boy B. a smart lad C. a lucky person D. a silent person

( ) 2. American and British English are two _____ of the English language.
    A. varieties B. elements C. parts D. forms

( ) 3. An unmarried lady is called Lucy Smith. How would you address her face to face?
    A. Lucy Smith B. Miss Lucy C. Miss Smith D. Darling

( ) 4. The following words are spelled typically in American English way except _____.
    A. color B. inquire C. judgement D. fulfill

( ) 5. Which of the following is an appropriate way to start a conversation?
    A. "It's snowing, isn't it?" B. "Where are you going, Bob?"
    C. "Going to classroom, Mary!" D. "It's really hot today, isn't it?"

( ) 6. Traditionally, culture contact consists of three forms. Which is wrong below?
    A. acquisition B. acculturation C. assimilation D. amalgamation

Chapter 11　Language and Culture

(　) 7. Nowadays a servant can be referred to as a _____.
　　A. sanitation engineer　　　B. beautician
　　C. landscape architect　　　D. domestic engineer

(　) 8. If your foreign teacher is called Black Clinton, the following ways to address him are acceptable except _____.
　　A. Mr. Clinton　　B. Black　　C. Mr. Black　　D. Sir

(　) 9. Which is not the component of culture?
　　A. language　　B. ideas　　C. belief　　D. soil

(　) 10. In a word, language express _____.
　　A. facts
　　B. events which represent similar world knowledge by its people
　　C. peoples' attitudes, beliefs
　　D. cultural reality

(　) 11. Which of the following proverbs was originated from Greece?
　　A. Sauce for the goose is sauce for the gander.
　　B. Too many cooks spoil the broth.
　　C. God helps those who help themselves.
　　D. Blood is thicker than water.

(　) 12. In a Western meal, you're offered a second helping, but you have already had enough. You would say _____.
　　A. No, thanks, I don't like it
　　B. No, I don't want any
　　C. No, I'm terribly full
　　D. That is delicious, but I've already had plenty, thanks

(　) 13. Which of the following is the right response of "Thank you"?
　　A. It doesn't matter.
　　B. Don't mention it. That's my duty.
　　C. Never mind.
　　D. That's all right.

(　) 14. _____ can be used as titles preceding surnames.
   A. "Judge"   B. "Manager"   C. "Teacher"   D. "Director"

(　) 15. Language is _____, which means that it is rule governed.
   A. arbitrary   B. systematic   C. vocal   D. symbolic

(　) 16. All the following things are valued in Western individualist culture except _____.
   A. self-reliance   B. equality of opportunity
   C. separateness   D. family duty

(　) 17. "I'm full." is signified in English culture by _____.
   A. an open hand, palm down, raised to one's throat
   B. one or both open hands lightly patting one's own stomach
   C. a raised open hand, palm forward
   D. moving quickly his open hand, palm down, across his throat

(　) 18. The inappropriate expressing of farewell for a western guest is _____
   A. I think I'd better be going now. I have got to get up early tomorrow.
   B. I think I ought to be going now. my baby sitter must leave at 11:00.
   C. I think I must be going now. I must not hold you any longer.
   D. I think I must be going now. I must have wasted you a lot of time.

(　) 19. _____ can be said as a reply to both thanks and apologies.
   A. "You're welcome."   B. "Don't mention it."
   C. "It's OK."   D. "That's all right."

(　) 20. The following are all swear words except _____.
   A. "Damn"   B. "Hell"   C. "Fuck"   D. "Death"

(　) 21. _____ may be used by racists to refer to Jews.
   A. "Japs"   B. "Dagos"   C. "Polacks"   D. "Kikes"

(　) 22. You can take a horse to the water, _____.
   A. but you cannot make him walk fast
   B. but you cannot make him run fast
   C. but you cannot make him drink
   D. but you cannot make him go back

Chapter 11 Language and Culture

( ) 23. "My hands are as cold as ice." is an example of _____.
A. similes   B. metaphors   C. proverbs   D. allusions

( ) 24. _____ is not euphemistic expression in English for lavatory.
A. "Comfort station"   B. "To be patient"
C. "To relieve oneself"   D. "To wash one's hands"

( ) 25. The most striking phonetic difference between American and British English is the pronunciation of _____ in words.
A. "r"   B. "a"   C. "wh"   D. "er"

( ) 26. Which idiom or saying below shows people's positive attitude towards dogs?
A. A jolly dog.   B. He worked like a dog.
C. Lead a dog's life.   D. Treat someone like a dog.

( ) 27. The most distinguishable linguistic feature of a regional dialect is its _____.
A. use of words   B. use of structures   C. accent   D. morphemes

( ) 28. "Surgical strike" is a euphemistic expression for _____.
A. "victory"   B. "invasion"   C. "military action"   D. "surprise attack"

( ) 29. When responding to compliment "You look very nice in this dress", you should say _____
A. "Thank you, but it is just so so."
B. "No, it is quite ordinary."
C. "Thank you. I'm glad that you like it."
D. "Do you really think so? I was not sure whether it suits me."

( ) 30. Sapir was an eminent anthropologist, whose ideas on language and thought was later developed by his student, B. L. Whorf, and is known as the Sapir-Whorf _____.
A. Theory   B. Hypothesis   C. Program   D. Method

( ) 31. Any linguistic sign may simultaneously have a _____
A. denotative   B. connotative
C. iconic   D. denotative, connotative, or iconic kind of meanings

(　) 32. _____ are the major source of regional variation of language.
　　　A. Geographical barriers
　　　B. Loyalty to and confidence in one's native speech
　　　C. Physical discomfort and psychological resistance to change
　　　D. Social barriers

(　) 33. After making an appointment, it is _____ people who are usually late.
　　　A. Chinese　　B. English　　C. German　　D. French

(　) 34. A meddlesome person who pries into others' affairs is called a _____.
　　　A. busman　　B. busybody　　C. ladies' man　　D. do-gooder

(　) 35. Which of the following groups are family names?
　　　A. Thomas, Richard, Robertson　　B. William, Smith, Clark
　　　C. Taylor, Anthony, Watkins　　D. George, Edwards, Jackson

V. Define the following terms.

taboos　　　　　　　　linguistic determinism　　　linguistic relativity
cultural diffusion　　　linguistic imperialism

VI. Answer the following questions briefly.

1. What is culture?
2. How would you define identity? How would you explain your identities to another person?
3. Give your culture's interpretation of the following nonverbal actions.
    (1) Two people are speaking loudly, waving their arms, and using many gestures.
    (2) A customer in a restaurant waves his hand over his head and snaps his fingers loudly.
    (3) An elderly woman dresses entirely in black.
    (4) A young man dresses entirely in black.
    (5) An adult pats a child's head.
    (6) Two men kiss in public.

Chapter 11 Language and Culture

4. How can studying the intercultural aspects of nonverbal behavior assist you in discovering your own ethnocentrism? Give personal examples.
5. Give a specific example of an intercultural communication experience in which an individual and/ or his or her culture might be harmed or changed.
6. Explain the strategies for intercultural communication.
7. How does a study of cultural values help you understand other cultures?
8. How can cultural differences in social perception affect the intercultural communication process?
9. Why is an awareness of identity important in your personal life? What are some of the situations in which this awareness would be beneficial?
10. How did you establish some of your identities? How do you enact those identities?
11. Discuss the following statement: "Prejudice can never be eliminated because it is so deeply rooted in human nature."
12. What do you think is the significance of culture teaching and learning?
13. What is meant by the following: "Most nonverbal communication is learned on the subconscious level."
14. Why is it useful to understand the nonverbal language of a culture?
15. What are some potential obstacles to accurately reading the nonverbal messages of other people?
16. Pick a foreign country in which you would like to study, do business, or visit. Find out as much as you can about that country's culture with regard to your purpose. For example, if you are going as a tourist, you might want to find out about table manners, medical emergencies, tipping, and so on.
17. How late can you be for the following: (a) a class, (b) work, (c) a job interview, (d) a dinner party, or (e) a date with a friend? Ask this same question of members of two or three cultures other than your own.
18. How many "brands" can you think of that have international recognition? What type of meaning (e.g., style, reliability, etc.) do you usually associate with those brands? Do other people assign the same meaning to them?

A Collection of Exercises in Linguistics

19. What are some of your different identities and how did you acquire them? What are some differences between your identities and those same identities in another culture?
20. What did linguists from the North American side do?
21. What is the relationship between language and culture?
22. Construction of a simple sentence in English is Subject–Verb–Object (S–V–O). In Japanese and Korean it is S–O–V. What kind of problems might this present for simultaneous translation?
23. Some scholars think the world is moving toward an "oligarchy" of major economic power languages. Do you think this would be a good or bad occurrence? Why? What will happen to minority languages, and what will be the result?
24. Differentiate and analyze linguistic relativity and the Sapir-Whorf Hypothesis.
25. Do we need culture in our linguistic study? Why?
26. What are the relative merits of a fundamentalist and a relativist approach to developing an intercultural ethic?
27. What are the three objectives for us to teach culture in our language class?
28. As a member of a host culture, what responsibilities do you believe you have to make immigrants feel comfortable in their new cultural environment?
29. Why is it said that much of culture is invisible?
30. Was the parenting style in your home more authoritarian or laissez-faire?
31. The section on Chinese history mentioned that Chinese officials were disturbed when British officials wore poppy flowers during a state visit. In your opinion, should the British representatives have worn the poppies? Why?
32. What are some of the communication challenges that will have to be managed over the next 50 years?
33. How to understand cultural Iceberg?
34. What is linguistic sexism?
35. How can a government use a nation's historical legacy to generate popular support among the general population?

36. Explain the statement: "Religion is only one kind of worldview."
37. What role might religion play in an intercultural communication encounter?
38. What cultural values help explain why face is more important in Asian societies than in the United States?
39. How do you think the United States becoming a "minority majority" nation will influence dominant culture values?
40. Explain what is meant by the phrase: "Communication is contextual." Can you think of examples of how context has influenced your behavior?
41. Do you believe mass media and social networking will make major alterations to gender roles in the next ten years? Why or why not?
42. What differences in behavior are exhibited by people who come from cultures that have different activity orientations?
43. Examine the concept of high- and low-context cultures. What problems can you anticipate when you are communicating with someone who holds a different context orientation?
44. What common set of ethics can you identify from the six religious traditions discussed in this chapter?
45. How does intercultural communication differ from everyday forms of communication?
46. What are some ways a person's family influences his or her cultural identity?
47. Examine the deep structure of your culture(s) and explain how it influences intercultural communication.
48. What images come to mind when you hear someone speaking English with an accent? Do different accents create different images? Try to decide why you form those images? Talk with others to see if they have the same experience.
49. Some countries have an official language (or languages), but others do not. What are the advantages and disadvantages of a country having an official language? Should the United States have an official language? Why?
50. What are the cultural differences between English and Chinese responses to compliments?

51. How can the historical legacies of the United States and Russia (China, Islamic nations) produce discord and conflict?
52. What is meant by "Nonverbal communication is rule-governed"?
53. According to the strong version of the Sapir-Whorf hypothesis, language determines speakers' perceptions and patterns their way of life. How in your view does language relate to thought and culture?

VII. Fulfill the following tasks.

1. List at least two occasions when you have experienced a consequence due to a communication.
2. Make a list of the changes in your culture that you have observed in your lifetime. Discuss with a group of your classmates how those changes have affected intercultural communication.
3. Identify the differences that exist between your various beliefs about the causes and treatment of illness and those found in another culture.
4. Interview someone from a culture different from your own using questions about child-rearing practices. You might inquire about methods of discipline, toys, games, topics discussed at the dinner table, and so forth. During the discussion share with them some "do's" and "don'ts" you were taught in your family.
5. In a group, identify and discuss the common principles and practices you see among all of the major religions.
6. Select a country (or culture) different from your own. Obtain as much information as you can about the history of that country. Try to isolate examples of how the country's national character has been determined by historical events.
7. Working with others, discuss the various ways the dominant culture influences and controls the values, attitudes, and behaviors of co-cultures.
8. Write down the different groups you belong to now and those you belonged to 4–5 years ago (include all informal groups, such as a study group). Compare your list with other classmates to see how frequently membership in a group has changed.

9. Attend a meeting (church service, lecture, social event, etc.) of a culture or co-culture different from you own. Try to notice the various ways cultural characteristics of that culture are being reflected in the interaction.
10. Working with others, think of some of the ways that the changing U.S. demography will likely affect your lives.
11. Explain the link between culture and communication.
12. Interview an older member of your family about the family's history. Try to identify a historical event that resulted in a family tradition carried on today.
13. Working with others, discuss the following question: "How does my view of death compare with the beliefs found in the six great religious traditions?" As part of your discussion, include observations on how a person's perception of death might influence his or her behavior.
14. Working with others, have each person discuss the "stories" that helped form his or her family and cultural identity.
15. Working with others, devise a plan that would reconcile the different learning preferences of students in a sixth-grade classroom with the following student balance: six Latinos, eight European Americans, five African Americans, four Japanese, and one Iranian.
16. In a class or online group, discuss the components of an intercultural ethic. How would you recommend that such an ethic be internalized so that it is always present during intercultural communication?
17. Meet with one or two ESL speakers to identify the kinship terms they use in their native language (e.g., mother, brother, aunt, etc.). Do they have kinship terms that vary with age differences? Do their kinship terms differ between own kin and other's kin? What cultural values do you think their terms reflect?
18. Working with others, discuss the following question: Are child-rearing practices throughout the world more alike than they are different?

A Collection of Exercises in Linguistics

19. Construct a list of as many of your identities as you can. Using the list, draw a pie chart with each identity receiving space proportional to that identity's importance to you. Compare your chart with other classmates' charts. Do members of the dominant and minority cultures differ in the amount of space allotted to their racial/ethnic identity? If so why?
20. Working with others, answer the following: "Why has religion been relevant to humankind for more than ten thousand years?"
21. Working with others, develop a protocol for entering into negotiations with a team of Brazilian, Chinese, or Indian negotiators. What considerations must you give to their business culture in developing your plan?
22. Looking back upon your school experiences, devise a plan to integrate the various cultures in a multicultural classroom into a classroom community.
23. Working with others and using Hofstede's value dimensions, make a list of behaviors found in American culture that reflect individualism, uncertainty avoidance, and femininity.
24. Working with some members of your class, try to compile a list of what you believe to be examples of American ethnocentrism.
25. What is the relationship among stereotypes, prejudice, racism, and ethnocentrism?
26. Talk with two or three people over sixty years of age and ask them for some examples of the slang they used in their younger days (e.g., "groovy man"). Try to compare it with slang that is popular now. You can also do this by watching a movie made before 1960.
27. Working with others, list the American cultural values. Try to think of other values that are not included in the text. Then find examples from American advertising campaigns that illustrate those values. For example, the advertising slogan, "Just do it." from an athletic-shoe manufacturer, reflects the American values of perseverance and accomplishment.
28. Interview people from other cultures and ask them if they have encountered communication problems when seeking health care.

Chapter 11 Language and Culture

29. Working with an ESL speaker, compile a list of animals that are common to both of you, then compare the sounds that each of you hear those animals make.
30. Attend an event—social, religious, etc.—populated by people from a culture different from your own. Make note of any differences between your culture and the culture you are visiting as they apply to greeting behavior, eye contact, voice volume levels, seating arrangements, dress, and the like.
31. Take four different English proper nouns (other than someone's name) and use online translation dictionaries to translate each noun into five different European languages. Do some of the translated nouns have a resemblance to the English nouns? If so, what are some possible reasons?
32. Locate pictures from magazines and newspapers that you believe are showing the following emotions through facial expressions: (a) anger, (b) joy, (c) sadness, (d) fear, and (e) revulsion. Show these pictures to people from various cultures and see what interpretations they give to the facial expressions.
33. Examine your worldview and determine how important spirituality is to your health care.
34. Watch a foreign film and look for examples of proxemics, touch, and facial expressions. Compare these to those of the dominant culture of the United States.
35. Working with others, determine some of the cultural problems that can arise in both a multinational and a domestic workforce. What are the problematic differences and similarities between the two workforces?
36. Working with others, make a list of typical American behaviors that relate to evil, good and evil, and good. How widespread are these behaviors within the culture?
37. Examine your behavior and determine how well you fit into the various degrees of time orientation.
38. Explain the phrase: "Our nonverbal actions usually reflect our culture."
39. Think about a recent conflict situation in which you participated (e.g., an argument with your significant other, your parents, or a stranger). What communication strategies did you use to give, maintain, or take face?

Chapter 12
Sociolinguistics
社会语言学

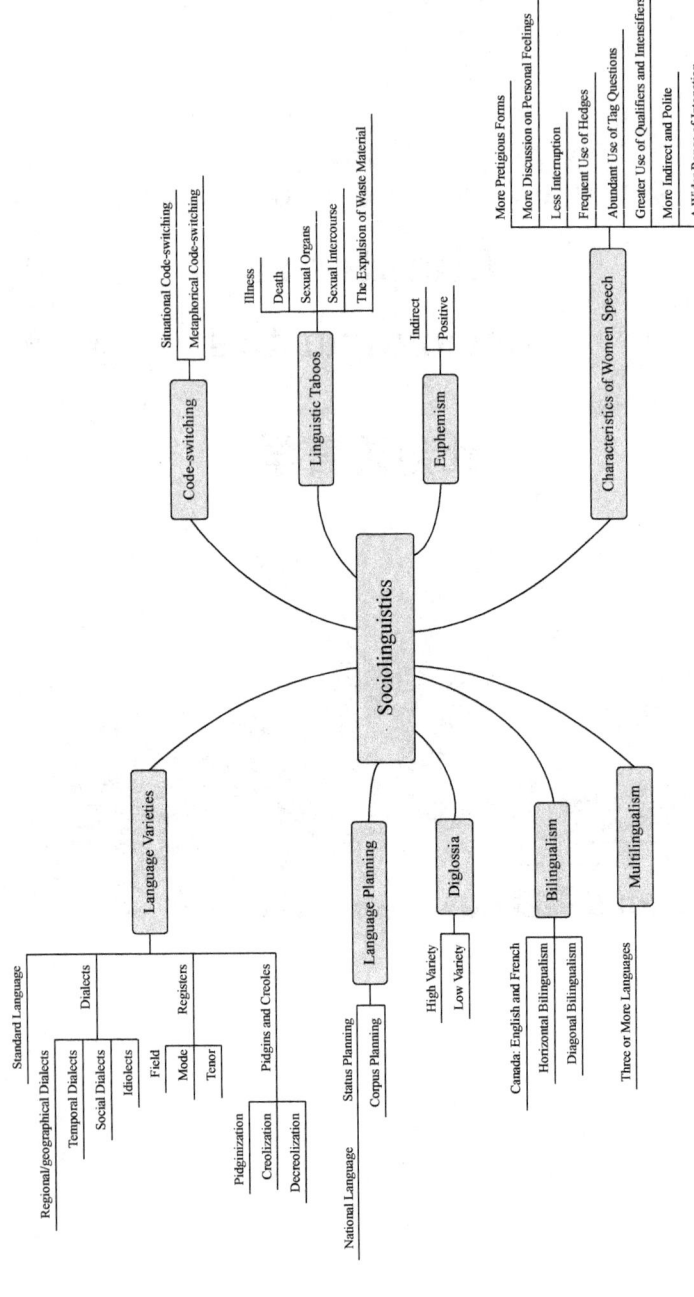

Figure 12 A Mindmap of Sociolinguistics

Chapter 12 Sociolinguistics

> **Key Points**
> Sociolinguistics is the study of the relationship between language and society. Two approaches to sociolinguistic studies: macro-sociolinguistics and micro- sociolinguistics

I. Decide whether each of the following statements is true or false.

(　) 1. Language reflects sexism in society. Language itself is not sexist, just as it is not obscene; but it can connote sexist attitudes as well as attitudes about social taboos or racism.

(　) 2. In socialinguistic studies, speakers are not regarded as members of social groups.

(　) 3. The sentences "He crazy" and "He be sick all the time" are both acceptable in Black English vernacular because copula deletion and habitual be are two famous features of Black English.

(　) 4. From the sociolinguistic perspective, the term "speech variety " can not be used to refer to standard language, vernacular language, dialect or pidgin.

(　) 5. Functional speech varieties are known as regional dialects.

(　) 6. It is generally accepted that the history of the English language is divided into the periods of Old English, Middle English and Modern English.

(　) 7. Standard American English is superior to Black English.

(　) 8. Geographical barriers are the only source of regional variation of language.

(　) 9. The standard language is a better language than nonstandard languages.

(　) 10. Sociolinguistics is the sub-discipline of linguistics that studies social contexts.

(　) 11. Language as a means of social communication is a homogeneous system with a homogeneous group of speakers.

(　) 12. Language use varies from one speech community to another, from one regional group to another, from one social group to another, and even from one individual to another.

( ) 13. A person's social backgrounds do not exert a shaping influence on his choice of linguistic features.

( ) 14. The goal of sociolinguistics is to explore the nature of language variation and language use among a variety of speech communities and in different social situations.

( ) 15. A lingua franca can only be used within a particular country for communication among groups of people with different linguistic backgrounds.

( ) 16. Bilingualism and diglossia mean the same thing.

( ) 17. The kind of name or term speakers use to call or refer to someone may indicate something of their social relationship to or personal feelings about that individual.

( ) 18. When people of a community speak the same language for different purposes, sociolinguistic situations known as diglossia and bilingualism emerge.

( ) 19. From sociological view we can derive meaning from context.

( ) 20. Women in Western countries at least appear to be more status-conscious and sensitive to the social significance of certain linguistic variables.

( ) 21. A pidgin usually reflects the influence of the higher, or dominant, language in its lexicon and that of the lower language in their phonology and occasionally syntax.

( ) 22. As language use is contextualized in particular social settings, social taboo originates from linguistic taboo.

( ) 23. Nonstandard languages are substandard languages.

( ) 24. In sociolinguistics, taboo denotes any prohibition on the use of particular lexical items to refer to objects or acts.

( ) 25. In medieval times, a trade language came into use in the Mediterranean ports. It consisted of Italian mixed with French, Spanish, Greek, Arabic, and Turkish, and it was called Lingua Franca, "Frankish language". The term lingua franca was generalized to other languages similarly used. Thus, any language can be a lingua franca.

Chapter 12 Sociolinguistics

(   ) 26. Some slang terms remain and become acceptable language used by the whole society.
(   ) 27. The territory in which the Indo-European languages are mainly spoken today also includes languages that are not Indo-European.
(   ) 28. The use of euphemisms has the effect of removing derogatory overtones and the disassociative effect as such is usually long-lasting.
(   ) 29. Black English is the widespread and familiar ethnic variety of the English language.
(   ) 30. A creole language is originally a pidgin that has become established as a native language in some speech community.
(   ) 31. A lingua franca must be a native language currently spoken by a particular people.
(   ) 32. The most distinguishable linguistic feature of a regional dialect is its grammar and uses of vocabulary.
(   ) 33. As pidgins are simplified languages with reduced grammatical features, they are in essence inferior to the English language.
(   ) 34. The linguistic markers that characterize individual social groups may serve as social markers of group membership.
(   ) 35. Sociolinguists are interested in "terms of address" because they offer some socio-cultural information about the type of relationship between the speaker and the hearer.
(   ) 36. Regional dialect is a variety of language related to the use of language.
(   ) 37. Two speakers of the same language or dialect use their language or dialect in the same way.
(   ) 38. Every speaker of a language is, in a stricter sense, a speaker of a distinct idiolect.
(   ) 39. Modern English began with the Norman Conquest.
(   ) 40. The division of English into Old English, Middle English, and Modern English is nonconventional and not arbitrary.

( ) 41. When people of a community speak the same language for different purposes, sociolinguistic situations known as diglossia and bilingualism emerge.

( ) 42. Diglossia refers to a sociolinguistic situation similar to bilingualism.

( ) 43. A linguistic taboo refers to a word or expression that is prohibited by the polite society from general use such as obscene, profane and swear words.

( ) 44. Idiolect is a personal dialect of an individual speaker that combines aspects of all the elements regarding regional, social and stylistic variation.

( ) 45. It is generally accepted that the history of the English language is divided into the periods of old English and modern English.

( ) 46. A child born to a Chinese or English speaking family takes about the same number of years to acquire their native tongue, regardless of their general intelligence.

( ) 47. Bilingualism describes a situation in which two very different varieties of language co-exist in a speech community, each with a distinct range of social function and appropriate for certain situations.

( ) 48. Euphemisms are created to replace taboo words or serve to avoid unpleasant subjects.

( ) 49. It has been noticed that in many communities the language used by the older generation differs from that used by the younger generation in certain ways.

( ) 50. It is an obvious fact that people who claim to be speakers of the same language don't speak the language in the different manner.

( ) 51. The protolanguage is the original form of a language family that still exists.

( ) 52. Shakespearian English belongs to Old English.

( ) 53. Dialectal synonyms can often be found in different regional dialects such as British English and American English but cannot be found within the variety itself, for example, within British English or American English.

(　) 54. Perfect bilingualism is uncommon because it is rare for individuals to be a perfect user of two languages in a full range of situations.

(　) 55. Pidgins are linguistically inferior to standard languages.

(　) 56. A regional dialect is a linguistic variety used by people living.

(　) 57. Linguistic taboo has nothing to do with social taboo.

(　) 58. The distinctive features of Black English persist for racial reasons.

(　) 59. Taboo refers to a descriptive term used in reference to words (or acts) that are not to be used (or performed) in "polite society".

(　) 60. In most bilingual communities, two languages have the same function in speech situations known as domains.

(　) 61. Micro-sociolinguistics is sociolinguistics proper.

(　) 62. The major difference between a pidgin and a creole is that the former usually has its native speakers while the latter doesn't.

(　) 63. An official language is in fact a national language.

(　) 64. Standard dialect is a particular variety of a language which any member of a speech community can possibly use regardless of his/her social and geographical backgrounds, his/her gender and age.

(　) 65. A pidgin is a special language variety that mixes or blends languages and it isn't used by people who speak different languages for restricted purposes such as trading.

(　) 66. It is interesting to know that the language used by men and women have some special features of others.

II. Fill in each of the following blanks with one word which begins with the letter given.

1. Language varieties other than the standard are called nonstandard, or v_____ languages.

2. Variation in language use associated with the sex of individual speakers is called g_____ varieties.

3. The original, or ancestral, form of a language family which has ceased to exist is called the p_____.
4. In many societies of the world, we find a large number of people who speak more than one language. As a characteristic of societies, b_____ inevitably results from the coming into contact of people with different cultures and different languages.
5. A p_____ is a special language variety that mixes or blends languages and it is used by people who speak different languages for restricted purposes such as trading.
6. The I_____ language family is the first and most widely investigated language family of the world.
7. Social variation gives rise to s_____ which are subdivisible into smaller speech categories that reflect their socioeconomic, educational, occupational background, etc.
8. The type of language which is selected as appropriate to the type of situation is r_____.
9. The avoidance of using taboo language mirrors social attitudes, emotions and value judgments and has no l_____ basis.
10. In sociolinguistic studies, speakers are treated as members of s_____.
11. The social group isolated for any given study is called the speech c_____.
12. Speech v_____ refers to any distinguishable form of speech used by a speaker or group of speakers.
13. From the sociolinguistic perspective, a speech variety is no more than a d_____ variety of a language.
14. A s_____ community is one group, all of whose members share the same language or at least a single language variety.
15. R_____ are situational dialects appropriate for use in particular situations; i_____ is a personal dialect.
16. S_____ is the sub-field of linguistics that studies the relation between language and society, between the uses of language and the social structures in which the users of language live.

17. The social group that is singled out for any special study is called the s_____.
18. A pidgin typically lacks in i_____ morphemes.
19. Linguistic taboo reflects s_____ taboo.
20. A d_____ is a linguistic variety used by people living in the same geographical region.
21. B_____ refers to a linguistic situation in which two standard languages are used either by an individual or by a group of speakers.
22. The standard language is a s_____, socially prestigious dialect of language.
23. S_____ variation in a person's speech or writing usually ranges on a continuum from casual or colloquial to formal or polite according to the type of communicative situation.
24. Language exists in time and changes through time. The description of a language at some point of time is called a s_____ study of language.
25. A regional dialect may gain status and become standardized as the national or o_____ language of a country.
26. Language standardization is also called language p_____.
27. An e_____ is a mild, indirect or less offensive word or expression substituted when the speaker or writer fears more direct wording might be harsh or unpleasant.
28. An excessive use of euphemism may have n_____ effects.
29. Dialectal diversity develops when people are separated from each other g_____ and socially. The changes that occur in the language spoken in one area or group do not necessarily spread to another.
30. Slang is often perceived as a low or vulgar form of language and is deemed to be undesirable in f_____ styles of language.
31. I_____ is a personal dialect of an individual speaker that combines aspects of all the elements regarding regional, social, and stylistic variation, in one form or another.
32. A c_____ language is originally a pidgin that has become established as a native language in some speech community.

A Collection of Exercises in Linguistics

III. Mark the choice that can best complete the statement.

( ) 1. _____ is concerned with the social significance of language variation and language use in different speech communities.
   A. Psycholinguistics   B. Sociolinguistics
   C. Historical linguistics   D. General linguistics

( ) 2. A speaker may change from the standard language to the non-standard language. This linguistic behavior is referred to as _____.
   A. language planning   B. speech change
   C. code-switching   D. bilingualism

( ) 3. _____ refers to the linguistic variety characteristic of a particular social class.
   A. Social-class dialect   B. Sociolect
   C. A and B   D. A or B

( ) 4. A linguistic _____ refers to a word or expression that is prohibited by the "polite" society from general use.
   A. slang   B. euphemism   C. jargon   D. taboo

( ) 5. The most distinguishable linguistic feature of a regional dialect is its _____.
   A. use of words   B. use of structures
   C. accent   D. morphemes

( ) 6. By studying sound correspondences from more languages, European linguists eventually ascertained that most languages of the languages of _____ belonged to the same Indo-European language family.
   A. Europe and the northern part of India
   B. Europe and Persia
   C. Persia and the northern part of India
   D. Europe, Persia and the northern part of India

Chapter 12　Sociolinguistics

(　) 7. _____ means that certain authorities, such as the government choose, a particular speech variety, standardize it and spread the use of it across regional boundaries.

　　A. Language interference　　　B. Language changes
　　C. Language planning　　　　　D. Language transfer

(　) 8. Depending on the demands of a particular communicative situation, bilingual or multilingual speakers may change between language varieties in the middle of speech or even in the middle of a sentence. Such a situation is known as _____.

　　A. bilingualism　B. multilingualism　C. diglossia　　D. code-switching

(　) 9. _____ refers to a marginal language of few lexical items and straight-forward grammatical rules, used as a medium of communication.

　　A. Lingua franca　B. Creole　　C. Pidgin　　D. Standard language

(　) 10. Modern English words man, woman, child, eat, fight, etc. originate from _____.

　　A. Middle English　　　　　　B. Old English
　　C. French　　　　　　　　　　D. Norman French

(　) 11. _____ in a person's speech or writing usually ranges on a continuum from casual or colloquial to formal or polite according to the type of communicative situation.

　　A. Regional variation　　　　　B. Changes in emotions
　　C. Variation in connotations　　D. Stylistic variation

(　) 12. _____ is speech variation according to the particular area where a speaker comes from.

　　A. Regional variation　　　　　B. Language variation
　　C. Social variation　　　　　　D. Register variation

(　) 13. A _____ is a variety of language that serves as a medium of communication among groups of people for diverse linguistic backgrounds.

　　A. lingua franca　　B. register　　C. creole　　D. national language

(　　) 14. Although _____ are simplified languages with reduced grammatical features, they are rule-governed, like any human language.
　　A. vernacular languages　B. creoles　C. pidgins　D. sociolects

(　　) 15. The important characteristic of a speech community is that the members of the group must, in some reasonable way, interact _____ with other members of the community.
　　A. geographically　　　　　B. linguistically
　　C. socially　　　　　　　　D. psycholinguistically

(　　) 16. _____ is the study of how language works in social interaction.
　　A. Sociolinguistics　　　　B. Psycholinguistics
　　C. Cognitive linguistics　　D. Neurolinguistics

(　　) 17. _____ belong(s) to the Indo-European language family.
　　A. English　B. German　C. French　D. All of them

(　　) 18. Which of the following statements is not the concern of sociolinguists?
　　A. The language a person uses reveals his social background.
　　B. There exist social norms that determine the type of language to be used on a certain occasion.
　　C. How does the human mind work when they use language?
　　D. To investigate the social aspects of language.

(　　) 19. In normal situations, _____ speakers tend to use more prestigious forms than their _____ counterparts with the same social background.
　　A. female, male　B. male, female　C. old, young　D. young, old

(　　) 20. _____ are the major source of regional variation of language.
　　A. Geographical barriers
　　B. Loyalty to and confidence in one's native speech
　　C. Physical discomfort and psychological resistance to change
　　D. Social barriers

(　　) 21. Which language family has the largest number of languages?
　　A. The Indo-European Family　　B. The Sino-Tibetan Family
　　C. The Austronesian Family　　　D. The Afroasiatic Family

(   ) 22. Which of the following belongs to the phonological features of Black English?

A. The frequent absence of various forms of the copular "be"

B. The use of double negation constructions

C. The deletion of some word-final stop consonants

D. All of the above

(   ) 23. The discovery of Indo-European language family began with the work of the British scholar _____.

A. Sir William Jones   B. John Firth

C. M. A. K. Halliday   D. F. D. Saussure

(   ) 24. A bilingual speaker often uses two languages alternatively during a conversation with another bilingual speaker, a speech situation known as _____.

A. discourse role-switching   B. activity role-switching

C. social role-switching   D. code-switching

(   ) 25. All the following languages belong to the Indo-European family except _____.

A. English   B. Chinese   C. German   D. French

(   ) 26. When a _____ comes to be adopted by a population as its primary language and children learn it as their first language, it becomes _____.

A. creole, pidgin   B. pidgin, reole

C. regional dialect, lingua franca   D. lingua franca, regional dialect

(   ) 27. Black English is a kind of _____ dialect.

A. regional   B. standard   C. ethnic   D. situational

(   ) 28. American Black English is _____.

A. a social variety   B. a regional variety

C. a combination of social and regional dialect   D. a temporal dialect

(   ) 29. The discovery of Indo-European began with the work of _____, who delivered an important paper in 1786 in which he suggested that Sanskrit bore a stronger affinity to Greek and Latin.

   A. the British scholar Sir William Jones

   B. the German linguist Franz Bopp

   C. the Danish scholar Rasmus Rask

   D. the German scholar Jacob Grimm

(   ) 30. Black English is probably the most widespread and most familiar _____ variety of the English language.

   A. regional   B. ethnic   C. social   D. lower class

(   ) 31. English-based pidgins are characterized by _____.

   A. an absence of any complex grammatical morphology

   B. a limited vocabulary

   C. both A and B

   D. none of the above

IV. Define the following terms.

sociolinguistics	speech community	speech variety
language planning	idiolect	standard language
nonstandard language	lingua franca	pidgin
creole	diglossia	bilingualism
ethnic dialect	sociolect	register
slang	euphemism	

V. Answer the following questions as comprehensively as possible. Give examples for illustration if necessary.

1. Discuss with examples that the speech of women may differ from the speech of men.

2. Excessive use of euphemism may have negative effects. Rewrite each of the following sentences to eliminate euphemistic expressions.

(1) The employees who had been notified of an interruption in their employment were referred to their outplacement manager.

(2) The official acknowledged that he had misspoken when he said the troops had not engaged in any protective-reaction missions.

(3) The prisoner's life will be terminated at dawn.

(4) The non-essential personnel in this division will be vacationed by next week.

(5) Reaching the top of the ladder of success must be a moving experience.

(6) I was told that he did away with himself.

(7) He'll be accountable despite his diabolical skill.

(8) It is a widespread but unproven hypothesis that the parameters of significant personal change for persons in mid-life are extremely narrow.

(9) I purchased a residential property that was in need of substantial upgrading.

3. Sociolinguistics aims to provide models of the communicative competence of members of a speech community. Discuss the factors which a sociolinguist must consider in attempting to achieve this aims.

4. Please analyze the regional dialect & sociolect.

5. How do you understand "Dialects of the same language sometimes are not mutually intelligible"?

6. Explain Dell Hymes' ethnographical framework.

7. A formal remark may have basically the same content as an informal one, but not necessarily the same social meaning. Write two directives and two statements with the same content but in two different register forms, each appropriate for a particular context.

8. What are the two major kinds of code switching?

9. Explain the differences between pidgin and creole and then specify their linguistic features respectively.

10. Change the following informal statements for formal situations.

(1) The delegates were savvy of the fact that the document they were signing wasn't perfect.

(2) The candidate slammed her opponent for often changing his tune on the issues.

(3) Stickley furniture may not be real smooth, but it's pricey and fresh.

11. What is a linguistic taboo? What effect does it have on our use of language?
12. How would you describe the diglossic situation in China?
13. Define standard and nonstandard language. Is standard language superior to nonstandard language?
14. What is bilingualism? What is a bilingual community? What does it mean that most bilingual communities have one thing in common?
15. Point out the marked differences between sociolinguistic study and traditional linguistic studies.
16. List several ways in which the speech of women and the speech of men differ from each other.
17. There are various suggestions why women tend to approximate more closely to the standard language than men do. What do you consider to be relevant factors? Why?
18. Describe three characteristics of Black English, including at least one phonological and one syntactic characteristic.
19. The following words are considered instances of sexist language. Find alternatives to these masculine-marked words.

    (1) businessman   (2) cleaning woman   (3) forefather   (4) housewife
    (5) kinsman   (6) layman   (7) spokesman   (8) statesman
    (9) stewardess   (10) workmanship

20. What distinction, if any, can you draw between bilingualism and diglossia?
21. What is language planning? Explain it with examples.
22. What are the two objectives of sociolinguistics?
23. Discuss with examples some of the linguistic differences between Standard English and Black English.
24. Explain bilingualism and multilingualism respectively.

Chapter 13
Psycholinguistics
心理语言学

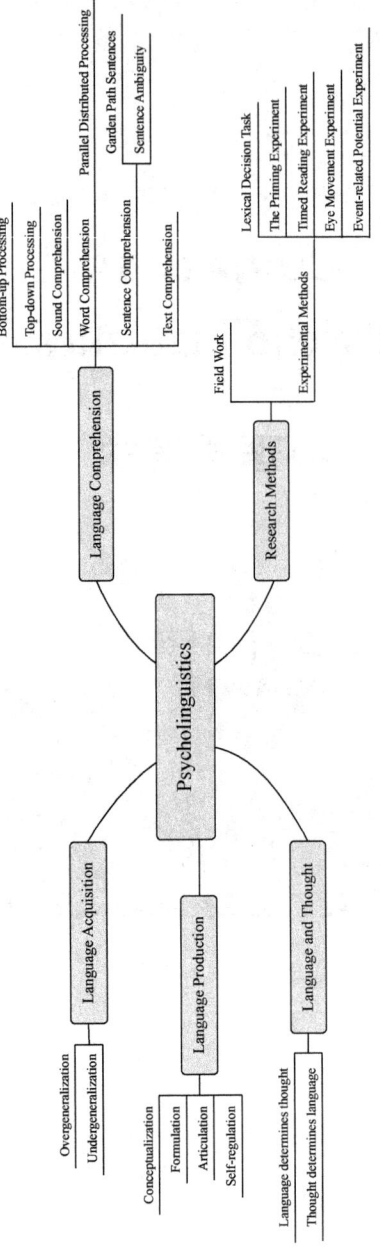

Figure 13 A Mindmap of Psycholinguistics

Chapter 13 Psycholinguistics

> **Key Points**
> Psycholinguistics is the study of language with reference to the workings of the mind.

I. Decide whether each of the following statements is true or false.

( ) 1. Psycholinguistics is said to be concerned with the use of language and speech as a window to the nature and structure of the human mind.

( ) 2. In terms of the cognitive function, the subject of a sentence is typically a coded search for some kind of existence or an agent in the world.

( ) 3. The "downhill" goal of psycholinguistics is to understand social experience about the referents of the words, but also a naturalization of the sense of the pragmatic strangeness.

( ) 4. The "uphill" goal of psycholinguistics is to understand the universal intelligent being.

( ) 5. The present goal of psycholinguistics is to discover the psychological processes that underpin the language use and development.

( ) 6. According to behaviorism, frequency plays a fundamental role in the patterns of human behavior.

( ) 7. In the psychology of language, a cognitive factor is a lower-level cognitive function that emerges as a condition that turns a feature/some features of linguistic performance on or off.

( ) 8. When we are interested in a topic, we know a lot about it and wish to know more.

( ) 9. For field workers in psycholinguistics, the objects of study distribute along the interactive domains rather than the autonomous domains.

( ) 10. Interactionism recognizes the child-environment interaction as important in accounting for the development of language.

( ) 11. The psycholinguistic methodology in general is typified by "introspection".

(　) 12. Intuitive analysis and topic analysis are both essential in developing the psycholinguistic expertise.

(　) 13. Developmental psycholinguistics examines how speech emerges over time and how children go about constructing the complex structures of their mother tongue.

(　) 14. Innatism holds that language acquisition does not depend totally on the influence of the environment.

(　) 15. In our intuitive framework for language production, the "downstream dragon" (the functional string of semantic modules) and the "upstream dragon" (the functional string of linguistic/syntactic modules) are attracted around the "ball" of the communicative intention in their functional uses of various cognitive resources.

(　) 16. In the present state of knowledge, psycholinguistic theories should be learned and memorized rather than institutionalized.

(　) 17. The data used for modeling the psychology of language include latency data, speech errors and true or false judgments.

(　) 18. Any recorded episode of children's language is useful data in the study of psycholinguistics.

(　) 19. Early psycholinguists were closely concerned with how autonomous or modularized language is.

(　) 20. A critical concern in psycholinguistics is with how the growing/developing child is cognitively conditioned in his or her language development.

(　) 21. Cognitive-functionally speaking, both language acquisition and use plausibly involve a grammar that is born in us.

(　) 22. "The child is the father of man" is the pertinent when we talk about the natural intelligence underlying language development and use.

(　) 23. Intuitively, the exceptional precocity of talented writers and speakers has provided excellent examples for us to draw psycholinguistic conclusions.

(   ) 24. One of the essential differences between chimps and human beings in communication is that the former do not have a complex fabric of social relations.

II. Mark the choice that can best complete the statement.

(   ) 1. Which of the following annotation is presently more appropriate for the question mark "?" in the following picture?

  A. "seeing"（看）

  B. "reading"（阅读）

  C. "visual input"（视觉输入）

  D. "visual pathway"（视觉通道）

(   ) 2. Which order there may be for the acquisition of the following words?

  A. big–small tall–short, long–short high–low thick–thin wide–narrow deep–shallow

  B. high–low thick–thin big–small tall–short long–short wide–narrow deep–shallow

  C. big–small high–low thick–thin wide–narrow deep–shallow tall–short long–short

  D. deep–shallow big–small tall–short, long–short high–low thick–thin wide–narrow

(   ) 3. Which of the following descriptions is not an appropriate one for child utterances?

  A. "telegraphic"

  B. "holophrastic"

  C. "overextended" or "underextended" in word meaning

  D. rule-governed

(   ) 4. The "slips of the tongue" are usually regarded as evidence for the cognitive processes in _____.

  A. language performance   B. language production

  C. language comprehension   D. language development

(   ) 5. It is said that one can see in "fool the pill for (fill the pool)" _____.
   A. the contrast between vowels and consonants in the minds of speakers
   B. the dissociation between linguistic knowledge and the language performance
   C. the similarities and differences between speech sounds
   D. the dissociation between sounds and meaning

(   ) 6. One-year-olds produce the so-called egocentric speech because _____.
   A. they talk about things around them as if they were the centers of their families
   B. they are in a transitional state of awareness of the world as if they were the center of all
   C. they are occupied or possessed by their own ego or concerns
   D. they are highly prejudiced

(   ) 7. The garden path model predicts that _____.
   A. people use purely syntactic information initially
   B. people use various clues at one go
   C. Semantic knowledge interacts with syntactic knowledge
   D. Semantic knowledge is used initially used

(   ) 8. Stephen Pinker's conceptualization of language instinct is a strong defendence of the view that _____.
   A. language is acquired in a universal pattern
   B. language is individually acquired
   C. language is acquired through children's interaction with their environment
   D. language is conditioned by outside stimulus

(   ) 9. Backtracking in speech is one of the many ways speakers edit their _____.
   A. linguistic performance   B. behavior
   C. thinking   D. words

Chapter 13　Psycholinguistics

(　) 10. Which of the following is not an appropriate title of a research paper?
　　　A. The kindergarten-path effect: studying on-line sentence processing in young children
　　　B. The learning in the maternal language environment
　　　C. How children make language out of gesture: Morphological structure in gesture systems developed by American and Chinese deaf children
　　　D. Opposing effects of age and reading ability on pseudoword priming

(　) 11. One way of discovering how we put words into our mouths is to look at _____ when we trip over our tongues.
　　　A. the time length　　　　　B. what happens
　　　C. the correction　　　　　D. the backtracking

(　) 12. The thematic roles include all of the following except _____.
　　　A. the agent　　　　　　　B. the theme
　　　C. the person　　　　　　D. the recipient

(　) 13. The correction of mistakes seems to have proved Chomsky's distinction between _____.
　　　A. competence and performance　B. knowledge and performance
　　　C. intuition and knowledge　　　D. reflex and intuition

(　) 14. The "uh" people often produce is a sign for _____.
　　　A. syntactic planning　　　B. hesitation
　　　C. correction of a mistake　D. erring

(　) 15. According to Scovel, children display an inborn sensitivity to the _____ of the language they are acquiring, as in the case of "up" in the following example.
　　　Child: Ben's picking up. He's hicking up.
　　　Adult: What?
　　　Child: He's got the hiccups.
　　　A. syntactic structures　　　B. the word meaning
　　　C. the thematic roles　　　D. the syntactic function of the word

163

( ) 16. Now we know that the over-regulated words such as goed and breaked are pieces of evidence for _____.
   A. creative language use   B. the application of empirical language rules
   C. linguistic imitations   D. childish use of language

( ) 17. _____ refers to the natural tendency of 6-month-old children to burst out in strings of consonant-vowel syllable clusters.
   A. Crying   B. Cooing   C. Babbling   D. gesturing

( ) 18. Parsing involves _____.
   A. the use of syntactic information
   B. the use of semantic information
   C. the use of both syntactic and semantic information
   D. the use of the language autonomy

( ) 19. There are two general trends in scientific thinking: _____.
   A. autonomy and interactionism
   B. modularity and constructionism
   C. innatism and interactionism
   D. subjectivity and objectivity

( ) 20. Most psycholinguists believe that the "foreign accents" of bilingual children at the age of 12 might suggest that there is a critical period that _____ determine first language learning.
   A. biologically   B. cognitively   C. innately   D. socioculturally

( ) 21. Chomsky proposed an innate LAD that allows children to constantly form and revise hypotheses on the basis of _____.
   A. output   B. native accent   C. innate knowledge   D. input

( ) 22. _____ is the study of language in relation to the mind.
   A. Psycholinguistics   B. Sociolinguistics
   C. Linguistics   D. Semantics

(   ) 23. Object permanence refers to the awareness of physical locations of objects around children, which supports the acquisition of such words as _____.

    A. mommy and daddy   B. allgone, gone, up and down
    C. doggie and kitty   D. this, the and a(n)

(   ) 24. At the age around 2 years old, the child has successfully acquired a vocabulary of _____.

    A. 50–200 words   B. 50 words
    C. 200 words   D. 1000 words

(   ) 25. At different ages, (usu. in terms of _____), children tend to pay attention to different aspects of language.

    A. weeks   B. months
    C. weeks and months   D. months and years

(   ) 26. _____, small children evoke a certain familiarity and directness not permissable with older children and adults.

    A. Ethnically   B. Sociolinguistically
    C. Psycholinguistically   D. Socially

(   ) 27. Perspective-taking is an important cognitive function after _____.

    A. communicative intention   B. topic selection
    C. pre-verbal message   D. syntactic planning

(   ) 28. Psycholinguistics is the study of _____ and mental activity associated with the use of language.

    A. psychobiology   B. psychological states
    C. physical states   D. biological states

(   ) 29. Early words are characterized by all the following except _____.

    A. phonetic easiness to pronounce
    B. morphological iconicity
    C. semantic abstractness
    D. situational function

(　　) 30. Which order does language follow in its development?

　　A. crying → babbling → cooing → one-word utterances → two-word utterances → questions → negatives → rare or complex constructions → mature speech

　　B. crying → cooing → babbling → one-word utterances → two-word utterances → questions → negatives → rare or complex constructions → mature speech

　　C. crying → cooing → one-word utterances → babbling → two-word utterances → questions → negatives → rare or complex constructions → mature speech

　　D. crying → cooing → babbling → one-word utterances → two-word utterances → negatives → questions → rare or complex constructions → mature speech

(　　) 31. The _____ model of learning words conveys the idea of acquiring simple words through a parent pointing at a dog and saying dog.

　　A. ostensive　　B. constructive　　C. behavioral　　D. the nativist

(　　) 32. Categorization is part of the _____ architecture of cognition.

　　A. functional　　B. environmental　　C. sociocultural　　D. innate

(　　) 33. Hearers perceive speech _____.

　　A. phonetically (sound by sound)

　　B. syllable by syllable

　　C. phonologically (with a specially phonological working memory)

　　D. phonemically (feature by feature)

(　　) 34. Which of the following statements about the brain function for language is presently more plausible?

　　A. The brain determines language.

　　B. The brain sub-serves linguistic interactions with our environment.

　　C. The brain is hard-wired for language.

　　D. The brain is an innate organ for language.

( ) 35. Selective attention to the stressed parts of the speech may help children acquire _____.
   A. syntax   B. early words   C. morphology   D. phonology

( ) 36. According to existing studies, the substitution of /l/ for /r/ in "a leading(reading) list" could happen probably because _____.
   A. the English language is organized
   B. it is difficult for people to distinguish between the two sounds
   C. the two sounds share many of the phonetic features
   D. sounds are dissociated from meaning

( ) 37. All of the following display structural ambiguities associated with parsing except _____.
   A. Boris said that Vlad finished it yesterday
   B. I saw the Alps flying to Romania
   C. Old men and women should get aboard right now
   D. The stone sings and dances

( ) 38. Levelt conceives speech production as a sequential process that include the following stages except _____.
   A. conceptualization   B. formulation
   C. self-regulation   D. articulation

( ) 39. Which order does the acquisition of the negative form may follow?
   A. I no want milk/I don't want milk. No singing song. I don't want some paper.
   B. I don't want some paper. No singing song. I no want milk/I don't want milk.
   C. No singing song. I no want milk/I don't want milk. I don't want some paper.
   D. I no want milk/I don't want milk. I don't want some paper. No singing song.

(　　) 40. A two-stage process for lexicalization involves _____.
　　　A. a) lemma selection (from the semantic level to an intermediate level of "lemmas（词条）" and b) retrieving the phonological forms of those words in the stage of phonological encoding (lexeme『词位』phonological form selection)
　　　B. a) lemmas are specified syntactically and b) the choice of a lemma
　　　C. a) lemma selection and b) lexeme selection
　　　D. a) lexeme retrieval and b) lemma specification

(　　) 41. "He swimmed in the pool" is usually _____.
　　　A. a children's error　　　　B. an adult error
　　　C. a language learner's error　D. an idiolect error

(　　) 42. Language production is often self-regulated with _____.
　　　A. language knowledge　　B. feedback loop
　　　C. grammar　　　　　　　D. meaning

(　　) 43. Conceptualization typically involves all of the following except _____.
　　　A. (speaker) conceiving the intention
　　　B. determining what to say
　　　C. selecting relevant information in preparation for construction of the intended utterance
　　　D. determining the appropriateness of the intended utterance

(　　) 44. Voice Onset Timing (VOT) is what people often attend to in _____.
　　　A. speech perception.　　　B. speech production
　　　C. parsing　　　　　　　　D. understanding of utterance meaning

(　　) 45. Categorical perception is the process of sound discrimination through _____.
　　　A. classification of sounds as belonging to sound or another
　　　B. the analysis of a distinctive feature
　　　C. the matching of one sample sound with the heard sound
　　　D. decisions based on probabilities

( ) 46. Parsing include all the following processes except _____.
   A. to determine the syntactic category to which each word in the sentence belongs (e.g. noun, verb, adjective, adverb, and so on)
   B. to combine those categories to form phrases
   C. to determine the subject of the sentence (what the sentence is about)
   D. to infer the speaker's intention

( ) 47. Sentence understanding involves _____.
   A. constructing a representation of the meaning of the sentence from such information about individual words
   B. inferring the speaker's intention
   C. finding out the word order
   D. dissolving the structural ambiguities

( ) 48. Crying is initially _____, because there is a direct link between the physical sound and its communicative intent.
   A. iconic   B. echoic   C. symbolic   D. holophrastic

( ) 49. Which of the following words are wrongly used in a present piece of psycholinguistic academic writing in the given sample.
   A central issue concerning the acquisition of verbs is whether verbs are semanticalized at any developmental stage.
   A. central   B. issue   C. whether   D. concerning

( ) 50. In structural ambiguity in the sentence "The horse raced past the barn fell" is described as _____.
   A. local ambiguity   B. permanent ambiguity
   C. global ambiguity   D. easy ambiguity

(   ) 51. The derivational theory of complexity (DTC) says that _____
   A. the more complex the formal syntactic derivation of a sentence — that is, the more transformations are necessary to form it — the more complex the psychological processing necessary to understand or produce it.
   B. transformationally complex sentences should be harder to process than generatively complex sentences.
   C. the parsing is easy for complex sentences.
   D. the meaning of complex sentences is accurately expressed.

(   ) 52. The canonical sentence strategy for parsing says all of the following except _____.
   A. we try the simpler strategies first
   B. if these do not work, we try other ones
   C. if the battery of surface structure strategies become exhausted by a sentence, we must try something else
   D. we must find the most efficient strategy for parsing

(   ) 53. Kimball's parsing strategy of right association means that _____.
   A. Our memory should not be over-loaded
   B. new words are preferentially attached to the lowest possible node in the structure constructed so far
   C. the sentence node takes up more memory capacity
   D. memory span is the most important constraint on parsing

(   ) 54. People can report what the omitted sound should be in the utterance "It was found that the eel was on the axle". This is taken as a piece of evidence for _____.
   A. the cognitive process of prediction of words according contextual cues
   B. the guessing of all words
   C. the insertion of sounds
   D. the unwanted use of sounds in language

Chapter 13 Psycholinguistics

(   ) 55. Which of the following contains information that should usually be included in an abstract?

A. The result seems to suggest that there are different contributing factors working towards the tuning of "goed" to "went".

B. The result is surprising.

C. We will describe a study that adopts an innate account of word selection.

D. Language acquisition is an important psycholinguistic topic.

(   ) 56. Formulation typically involves translating the conceptual representation into a linguistic form through _____.

A. forming an intention

B. selecting words (lexicalization)

C. syntactic planning (to put words together to form sentences)

D. detailed phonetic and articulatory planning

E. Phonological encoding (words into sounds)

(   ) 57. For the sentence "Vlad figured that Boris wanted to take the pet rat out", the right-association strategy says that the word "out" is _____.

A. directly attached to rat

B. more closely attached to "take" rather than to "figured"

C. preferably attached to "figured"

D. preferably attached to "wanted"

(   ) 58. The constraint-based model uses all of the following information except_____.

A. Syntactic information

B. semantic information

C. contextual cues and frequency

D. morphological information

A Collection of Exercises in Linguistics

(　) 59. The Parallel Distributed Processing (PDP) perspective argues that _____.

    A. our understanding of speech goes on in several stages

    B. we use several separate but simultaneous processes in understanding language

    C. there is the cooperation between different parts of our brain

    D. we use different processes on a single analytic level of language

(　) 60. A logogen in the mental lexicon is _____.

    A. a lexical detection device for a word in the processes of speech comprehension

    B. a sign that can be fired in the neurological organization of words

    C. a word that arranges itself with other words

    D. a process that tries to directly find the meaning of the heard word

(　) 61. A hypothesis in psycholinguistic experiments is a tentative representation of the relation between _____.

    A. two variables

    B. two independent variables

    C. a dependent variable and an independent variable

    D. two independent variables

(　) 62. A psycholinguistic "account" can be described by all the following except _____.

    A. It must agree with the opinion of a psycholinguistics student

    B. It tentatively explains of the result of hypothesis test

    C. Its explanation helps the choice of a plausible theory

    D. The account should be easily unified with other accounts if there is any

    E. It must be able to yield a deeper understanding of the reality

( ) 63. Which of the following sounds more like a sentence that would appear at the beginning of a research paper?
   A. Chomsky, the famous linguistics professor MIT, has provided an innate account for language acquisition.
   B. Nowadays, people are using English more and more frequently across different cultural backgrounds.
   C. An important issue concerning language acquisition is what contributes to the formal system of child language.
   D. As is known to all, language acquisition is a process that involves many influences.

III. Define the following terms.

psycholinguistics	cerebral cortex	brain lateralization
linguistic lateralization	dichotic listening	the critical period
intrapersonal communication	subvocal speech	

IV. Answer the following questions.

1. Consider the following slips of tongue. What does each reveal about the process of language production?
   (1) They laked across the swim.
   (2) The spy was gound and bagged.
   (3) I will zee you in the bark.
2. Words in our mental lexicon are known to be related to one another. Discuss the relationships between words, using examples from the English language.
3. Imagine that the following nonwords are nouns in English: juld, sprenk, spluce, plize, merket, crox, smarg. What would the plurals of these nonwords be, in their spoken form? See if other native speakers agree with you. What does this tell you about the process of making plurals in English?

A Collection of Exercises in Linguistics

4. Newspaper headlines are often incomplete sentences or leave out shorter or less important words. This can result in unintended amusing or ambiguous results, as in "Man gets nine years in violin case." or "Sisters reunited after twenty years in checkout queue." Look out for such instances when you read newspapers, and try to work out why the headlines have the effect they do. Alternatively, Google "Amusing headlines" to find a number of collections. Think about what it is that we do when we read texts that result in such amusing interpretations.

5. Sentences (1) and (2) below contain words from four grammatical categories: nouns, verbs, determiners and prepositions. Replace the words in each sentence with their grammatical category labels. Each sentence contains a prepositional phrase that modifies some other part of the sentence. Underline the prepositional phrases, and taking plausibility into account, put a box around the word that you think the prepositional phrase in each sentence modifies.

    (1) The spy saw the cop with the binoculars.

    (2) The spy saw the cop with the revolver.

6. What are the uniqueness points of the words *monkey* and *swing*? In the sentence context below, is the recognition point for each word likely to be the same as its uniqueness point? Justify your answers by saying what kinds of information might be used in recognising the words. All the children loved watching the long-tailed monkey as it started to swing through the trees.

7. Explain coherence and cohesion with reference to the passage in (1) below, and use these concepts to show why the passage in (2) does not work.

    (1) The blonde girl immediately fell asleep. When the bears returned to their cottage, they saw that she had been eating their porridge.

    (2) Cinderella watched the prince ride up to her house. The prince tied it up and he sacked his servants.

8. What sort of word-level error has taken place in the following examples?

    (1) to determine what/which. to determine watch (Fromkin, 1973a)

    (2) a branch falling on the roof. a branch falling on the tree (Fromkin, 1973a)

    (3) a language learner needs. a language needer learns (Fromkin, 1973a)

Chapter 13　Psycholinguistics

(4) chamber music. chamber maid (Fromkin, 1973a)

(5) wine is being served at dinner. dinner is being served at wine(Fromkin, 1973a)

(6) many players think... many people think he's the most underrated player in the nation (FSED)

9. Describe the processes of language perception, comprehension and production.
10. What are the deviation points of the following nonwords?
    blorsilize   breganist   brondation   munart   pytel   shrortile
11. Work out how many orthographic neighbors (words differing by one letter) the following words have, and place them in two groups of three words according to neighbourhood size:
    bash   deem   lust   maul   mope   romp
    Given that all these words have quite low frequencies of use, what outcome would you predict for the relative speed of naming them (reading them out loud)? What about for their speed of recognition in a task like progressive embarking?
12. Re-write the sentences below with subscripts to show the links between anaphors and their antecedents.
    (1) Bert asked Ernie to lend him some money.
    (2) John and Mary stayed until she had finished checking the book for him.
    (3) Joan complained to her parents that they never let her go out on her own.
    (4) Spike promised John that he would finish the job.
    (5) Spike persuaded John that he should finish the job.
13. If you find yourself (or a conversational partner) in a tip-of-the-tongue state i.e. you know there is a word for what you want to say but you just can't find it, then write down what you (or the speaker if it is not you) can remember about the word. i.e. how long the word is, what kinds of sounds it has, what the stress pattern of the word is, what other words are similar in sound or meaning. If you subsequently are able to recall the word, how much overlap does it have with the characteristics you were able to remember?

14. Underline the subject and draw a box around the object in each of the following sentences.

    (1) The man bought the CD.

    (2) The very suspicious but rather inexperienced spy used the binoculars.

    (3) The dog chased the cat that had recently brought a mouse into its owners house.

15. Underline the fillers and indicate the gaps in the following sentences, using underscores and subscripts where necessary.

    (1) Who did Mary ask to meet John?

    (2) Who did Mary ask John to meet?

    (3) Which book did you persuade John to read during the holiday?

    (4) What did you pack to take on holiday?

    (5) Which book did the choir sing that carol from?

16. In what cortical regions are speech and language thought to be localized?

17. All of the following sentences are grammatically correct. Imagine that an experimental task is to match each sentence to a picture showing the situation described in the sentence, where that picture is one of a set of pictures showing different things. For each sentence, would you predict the sentence-picture matching to be straightforward if the syntactic analysis system was restricted to (a) subject–verb–object ordering of content words with no further grammatical information, (b) no grammatical information at all?

    (1) The boy stroked the cat.

    (2) The dog chased the cat.

    (3) The parcel was opened by the teacher.

    (4) The woman read the book.

    (5) The table was polished by the cleaner.

    (6) The tailor mended the coat.

18. Describe one research technique that has provided linguists with information about the localization of speech and language in the brain.

19. Give a rank ordering for the sentences below in terms of their grammaticality. What properties of the sentences do you think led you to give them that rank ordering?
    (1) The postman delivered the junk mail threw it in the trash.
    (2) The tenant delivered the junk mail threw it in the trash.
    (3) Postmen delivered the junk mail threw it in the trash.
    (4) Tenants delivered the junk mail threw it in the trash.
20. Many left-handed people have their language centers in the right hemisphere of the brain. What type of result would we expect to obtain from such people on a dichotic listening task?
21. Provide evidence for the view that there is a critical period for language acquisition.
22. What is the subordination index of the following sentences?
    (1) Because he was convinced she liked it, the man bought his wife a CD of a symphony they had heard on the radio.
    (2) They listened to it the next day.
    (3) She took it back because it was not the symphony they had heard.
    (4) The shop replaced it with the one the man should have bought.
23. What sort of paralexias are involved when a patient says (a) dad when reading the word 〈father〉, (b) tantrum for 〈tandem〉, (c) scent for 〈perfect〉 (d) helpless for 〈helpful〉?
24. buffalo buffalo buffalo buffalo buffalo buffalo buffalo is, surprisingly, a well-formed sentence of English. Add explicit markers to make the meaning clear. Note that the word buffalo has multiple uses:
    (1) a type of cattle
    (2) a city in New York state
    (3) a verb use, meaning to bully.
25. What sort of gestural patterns would you expect native speakers of each language to use when saying the sentence in their language?

26. Think of two places you might want to get to from your home. Ask someone who lives with you to describe the route to each of these places. For the first description, don't give your informant any further instruction. For the second one, tell them to do this while sitting on their hands or holding their hands behind their backs. Do you notice any difference in their fluency? Do they report finding one task any easier to complete than the other?

27. Based on the first two sounds (phonemes) of the words *monkey* and *swing*, what words are in the word-initial cohort of each?

28. The perceptual integration of visual and auditory inputs known as the McGurk effect is a powerful effect. Would you expect it to happen if the face you see is clearly not the origin of the voice you hear (e.g. if the face is female and the voice is male)?

29. According to the strong version of the Sapir-Whorf hypothesis, language determines speakers' perceptions and patterns their way of life. How in your view does language relate to thought and culture?

30. Draw syntactic tree structures to show the two structures involved for each of the following ambiguous sentences.

    (1) I saw the astronomer with a telescope.

    (2) I saw the book that you were reading in the library.

    (3) Fred realized that Mary left when the party started.

Chapter 14
Neurolinguistics
神经语言学

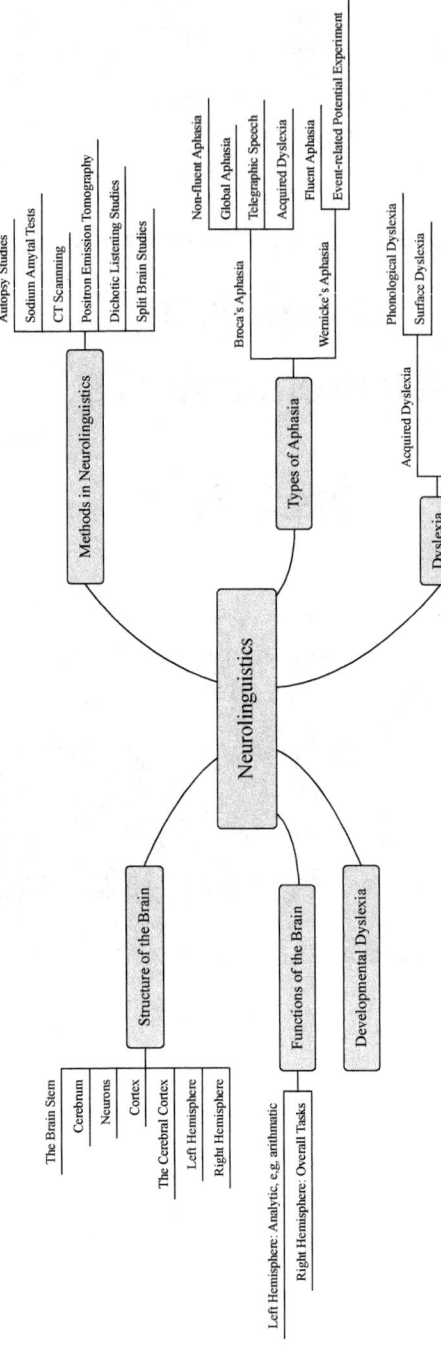

Figure 14 A Mindmap of Neurolinguistics

Chapter 14 Neurolinguistics

> **Key Points**
> Neurolinguistics is the study of two related areas: language disorders and the relationship between the brain and language.

I. Decide whether each of the following statements is true or false.

(   ) 1. Evidence in support of lateralization for language in left hemisphere comes from researches in Dichotic listening tasks.

(   ) 2. Psychological research suggests that the left hemisphere is superior to the right hemisphere because left brain controls language and analytic reasoning.

(   ) 3. In general, the right hemisphere of brain controls the right side of the body, the left hemisphere of the brain controls the left side of the body.

(   ) 4. The angular gyrus is the language center responsible for converting a visual stimulus into an auditory form and vice versa.

(   ) 5. Research findings have shown that language processing centers are situated in a single area of the left hemisphere.

(   ) 6. The left hemisphere of the brain is superior to the right hemisphere because the left hemisphere is language-dominant.

(   ) 7. Generally speaking, left hemisphere is responsible for language and speech, analytic reasoning, associative thought, etc., while the right hemisphere is responsible for perception of nonlinguistic sounds, holistic reasoning, recognition of musical melodies, etc.

(   ) 8. Generally speaking, left-handed people have their language centers in the left hemisphere of the brain.

(   ) 9. The brain is divided two sections: the higher section called the brain stem and the lower section called the cerebrum.

( ) 10. Dichotic Listening is a research technique which has been used to study how the brain controls hearing and language, with which subjects wear earphones and simultaneously receive different sounds in the right or left ear, and are then asked to repeat what they hear.

( ) 11. An interesting fact about these two hemispheres is that each hemisphere controls the opposite half of the body in terms of muscle movement and sensation.

( ) 12. Most right-handed individuals are said to be right lateralized for language.

( ) 13. Recognition of patterns is a mental function in the left hemisphere of the human brain.

( ) 14. Participating in the processes of language perception, comprehension and production are just a number of brain areas called language centers.

( ) 15. Neurolinguistics is the study of two related areas: language disorders and the relationship between the brain and language.

( ) 16. Linguistic lateralization in terms of right hemispheric dominance for language is found to exist in an overwhelming majority of human beings.

( ) 17. Linguistic lateralization is hemispheric specialization or dominance for language.

( ) 18. Right hear advantage shows the right hemisphere is not superior for processing all sounds, but only for those that are linguistic in nature, thus providing evidence in support of view that the left side of the brain is specialized for language and that's where language centers reside.

( ) 19. CT scanning uses a narrow beam of X-ray to create brain images that take the form of a series of brain slices.

II. Fill in each of the following blanks with one word which begins with the letter given.

1. The brain is divided into two roughly symmetrical halves, called h_____, one on the right and one on the left.

2. The cortex has many wrinkles: a ridge (hill) on the cortex is called g_____; a groove (valleys) on the cortex is called sulcus and a deep and prominent sulcus is called fissure.
3. Brain l_____ is the localization of cognitive and perceptual functions in a particular hemisphere of the brain.
4. By means of d_____ listening tests, we can analyze the characteristics of incoming stimuli processed by the individual hemispheres.
5. The n_____ view of language acquisition is that humans are equipped with the neural prerequisites for language and language use, just as birds are biologically "prewired" to learn the songs of their species.
6. C_____ cortex is the outside surface of the brain which receives messages from all the sensory organs and where human cognitive abilities reside.
7. Each hemisphere is conventionally divided into four lobes: f_____, parietal lobe, temporal lobe and occipital lobe.
8. Language functions are believed to be lateralized primarily in the l_____ hemisphere of the brain.
9. Neurolinguistics is the study of two related areas: language disorders and the relationship between the b_____.
10. The brain's neurological specialization for language is called linguistic l_____, which is specific to human beings.

III. Mark the choice that can best complete the statement.

( ) 1. What cortical region(s) are speech and language thought to be localized?
    A. Broca's area   B. Wernicke's area
    C. the angular gyrus   D. All of the above

( ) 2. Psychologists, neurologists and linguists have concluded that, in addition to the motor area which is responsible for physical articulation of utterances, three areas of the left brain are vital to language, namely, _____.
A. Broca's area, Wernicke's area and the angular gyrus
B. Broca's area, Wernicke's area and cerebral cortex
C. Broca's area, Wernicke's area and neurons
D. Broca's area, Wernicke's area and Exner's area

( ) 3. Which of the following mental functions is not under the control of the left hemisphere?
A. Language and speech   B. Analytic reasoning
C. Holistic reasoning   D. Calculation

( ) 4. Difficulty in language comprehension may be caused by _____.
A. damage to the Broca's area
B. damage to the Wernicke's area
C. damage to the arcuate fasciculus
D. damage to the angular gyrus

( ) 5. Damage to parts of the left cortex behind the central sulcus results in a type of aphasia called _____.
A. Wernicke's aphasia   B. Broca's aphasia
C. acquired dyslexia   D. fluent aphasia

( ) 6. _____ uses a narrow beam of X-ray to create brain images that the form of a series of brain slices.
A. PET   B. MRI   C. CT scanning   D. fMRI

( ) 7. The angular gyrus is crucial for _____.
A. the matching of a spoken form with a perceived object
B. the naming of objects
C. the comprehension of written language
D. all of the above

Chapter 14 Neurolinguistics

(　　) 8. Inability to repeat what is heard may be caused by _____.
   A. damage to the Broca's area　　B. damage to the Wernicke's area
   C. damage to the arcuate fasciculus　D. damage to the angular gyrus

(　　) 9. The brain is divided into two sections: the lower section called the _____ and the higher section called the _____.
   A. brain stem, cerebrum　　　B. brain stem, neurons
   C. cerebrum, brain stem　　　D. cerebrum, neurons

(　　) 10. Which of the following choices is not the key biological basis for human language acquisition?
   A. Cerebral cortex   B. Neurons   C. Eyes   D. Angular gyrus

(　　) 11. Difficulty in speech production may be caused by _____.
   A. damage to the Broca's area
   B. damage to the Wernicke's area
   C. damage to the arcuate faciculus
   D. damage to the angular gyrus

(　　) 12. _____ is the language center responsible for converting a visual stimulus into an auditory form and vice versa.
   A. The angular gyrus　　　B. Broca's area
   C. Wernicke's area　　　　D. None of the above

(　　) 13. Which of following is a correct annotation for the "marked area in the brain"?
   A. the Broca's area　　　B. the Wernicke's area
   C. the arcuate faciculus　D. the angular gyrus

(　　) 14. Which of the major mental functions listed below is not under the control of the left hemisphere in most people?
   A. language and speech　　B. visual and spatial skills
   C. reading and writing　　　D. analytic reasoning

IV. Define the following terms.

interlanguage	affective filter	acquired dyslexia
Broca's area	Wernicke's area	Wernicke's aphasia
dichotic listening	cortex	temporal lobe
lateralization	hemisphere	

V. Answer the following questions briefly.

1. What is neurolinguistics?
2. Why is it thought that speech and language function may not be cognitively unique?
3. In what cortical regions are speech and language thought to be localized?
4. What is linguistic context and what is physical context? Give an example to illustrate.
5. How does the brain encode and decode speech and language?
6. Are the components of language neuroanatomically distinct?
7. What abilities does Aptitude Test try to measure?

Chapter 15
Corpus Linguistics
语料库语言学

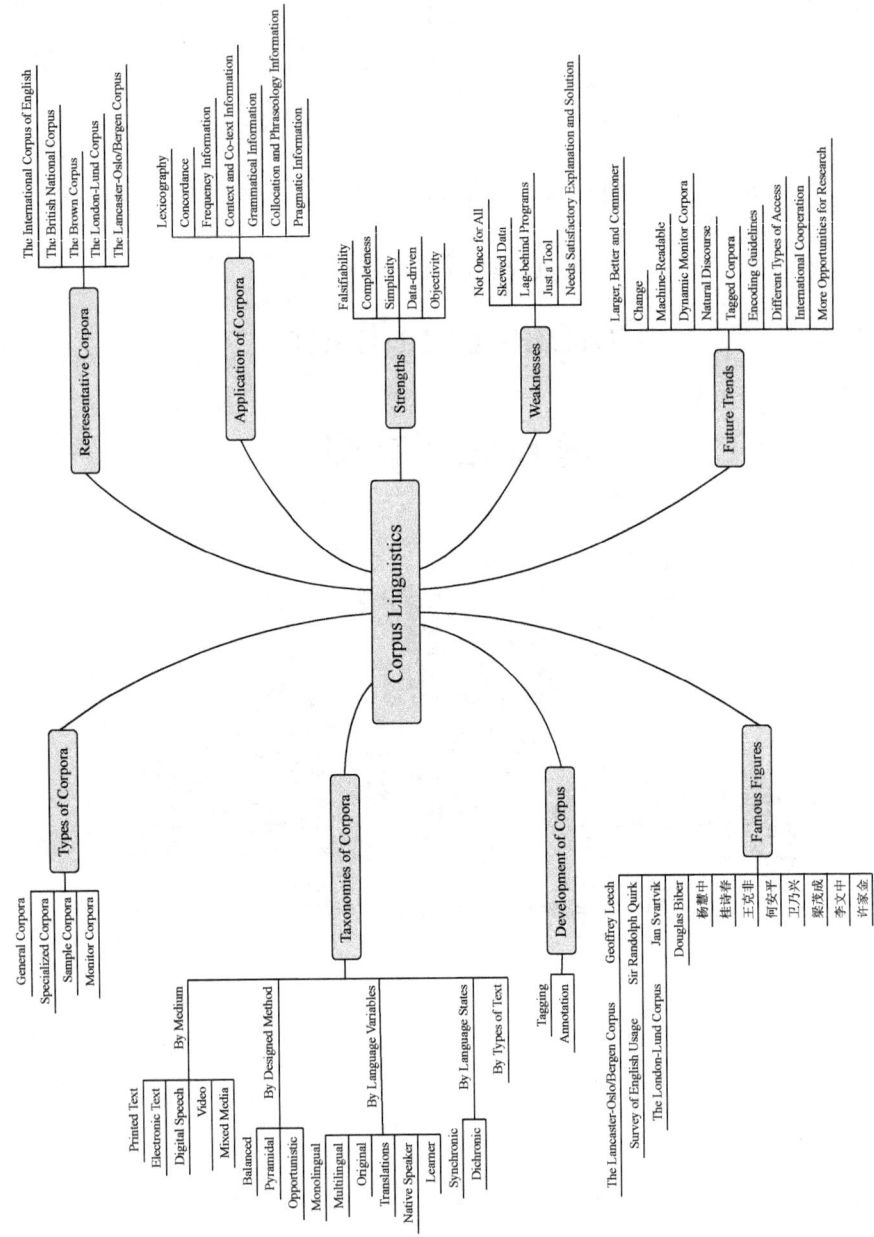

Figure 15 A Mindmap of Corpus Linguistics

Chapter 15 Corpus Linguistics

> **Key Points**
> Corpus Linguistics is an approach to investigate language that is characterized by the use of large collections of texts (spoken, written or both) and computer-assisted analysis methods.

I. Define the following terms.

corpus   annotation   concordance
word frequency   token

II. Answer the following questions briefly.

1. How do spoken and written registers differ in their use of dependent clauses?
2. How can the use and function of grammatical classes be better understood by analyzing their distribution across registers?
3. How is speech different from writing in English? Specifically, what patterns in the use of linguistic features are important in distinguishing among the major spoken and written registers?
4. How have written and speech-based registers changed in their linguistic characteristics over the last three centuries?
5. How are seemingly synonymous words used and distributed in different ways?
6. How can nearly synonymous words, with the same grammatical potential, be distinguished in terms of use patterns relating to their grammatical associations?
7. What is the frequency of a word relative to other related words?
8. What linguistic and non-linguistic features are associated with the choice between seemingly synonymous structural variants?
9. What are the two principles for word collocation put forward by Sinclair?
10. What words commonly co-occur with a particular word, and what is the distribution of these "collocational" sequences across registers?
11. What factors should we consider if we are asked to design a corpus?
12. What are the linguistic characteristics of fifth-grade spoken and written registers?

13. How are the senses and uses of a word distributed?
14. How can the function of syntactic constructions be better understood by analyzing their distribution and linguistic associations across registers?
15. How do the error patterns of non-native English speakers compare to those of native speakers?
16. How can the use of nearly synonymous grammatical constructions be understood in terms of their differing lexical associations?
17. How are references marked in different ways in different kinds of texts?
18. What are the linguistic characteristics of particular texts written by an author, when considered relative to a range of other texts from the same period?
19. How can the use and function of morphological characteristics be better understood by analyzing their distribution across registers?
20. How does the sequence of verbs within a text develop with respect to the marking of tense and voice?
21. Considering individual linguistic features, how does written proficiency develop from third to sixth grade?
22. How are specific spoken and written registers similar or different in terms of those patterns?
23. What are the main functions of corpora or corpus linguistics as far as you know?
24. What are the features of corpus linguistics?
25. In what ways does the language of elementary students develop from third to sixth grade?
26. In what ways are the dimensions of variation for fifth-grade language similar to and different from the dimensions of variation for adult language?
27. How do texts from different academic disciplines vary with respect to patterns of linguistic variation?
28. How do the internal sections of texts within a single academic register vary linguistically?
29. What are the seven maxims of annotation?
30. What are the meanings associated with a particular word?

31. What non-linguistics association patterns does a particular word have (e.g. to registers, historical periods, or dialects)?
32. How have the patterns of use for modal verbs versus semi-modal verbs shifted over the last three centuries (in the domain of obligation/necessity modality)? In addition, do the patterns of use for individual verbs differ from these overall patterns?
33. Design a research project, using data from a corpus. The main content of your project shall include research questions and research methodology.

Chapter 16
Stylistics

文体学

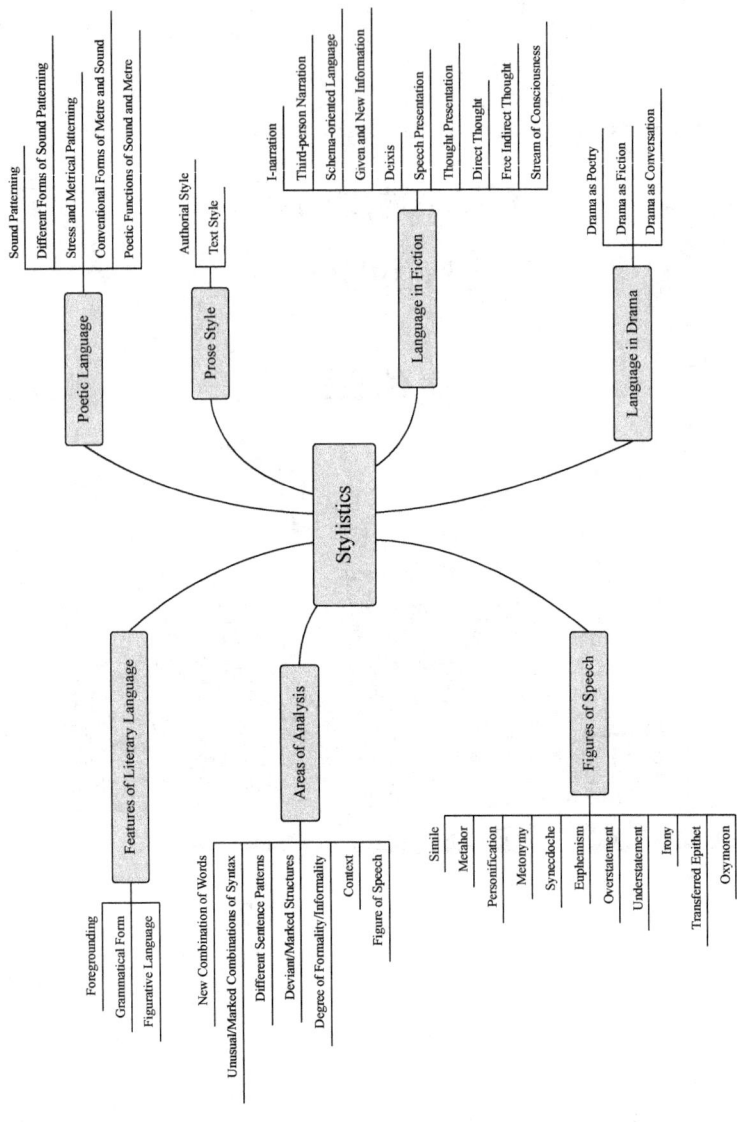

Figure 16 A Mindmap of Stylistics

Chapter 16 Stylistics

> **Key Points**
> Stylistics is the study of the use of language in literature. It takes literary discourse as its object of study and uses linguistics as a means to that end.

Ⅰ. **Decide whether each of the following statements is true or false.**

(　) 1. Simply speaking, registers refer to languages which are determined by situation.

(　) 2. Exophora is an item that refers to something in another text.

(　) 3. Euphemism is a kind of mild expression for an offensive or harsh one.

(　) 4. Taboo refers to words forbidden to be used in public because of their being dirty or offensive.

(　) 5. Pause can be divided into structural pause and emotive pause.

(　) 6. Intimate style is usually used between husband and wife. Moreover, it is employed in jargons sometimes.

(　) 7. Tenor of discourse is the social relationships between the participants in the communication.

(　) 8. Lexical analysis is chiefly concerned about how the words in a text are put together to produce meaning and other kinds of message.

(　) 9. Rhetorical question is a question which does not need an answer or the answer is obvious.

(　) 10. Contrastive conjunction is achieved by the use of conjunctive words of addition or progression, such as *and, furthermore, moreover,* etc.

(　) 11. Loose sentence is one that is not grammatically complete until the end is reached.

(　) 12. The compositions written by a class of middle school students can be called different styles.

(　) 13. Content is the style that may be different from case to case although the meaning may remain the same.

(　) 14. Repetition is a rhetorical device in which two or more than two similar syntactic structures with different words are placed side by side.

(　) 15. In this example: "Is this a non-smoker? I don't know", there is a verbal ellipsis.

(　) 16. A not-text is a group of sentences that are typically or logically linked together. This kind of linkage is called cohesion. So cohesion is the quality that makes a text a text.

(　) 17. Syntactical analysis is chiefly concerned about how sentences are joined together to produce a cohesive and coherent text.

(　) 18. The British English word "autumn" and the American English word "fall" are called stylistic synonyms.

(　) 19. Idiolect is the stylistic variation in a person's speech, or writing, usually ranges on a continuum from casual or colloquial to formal or polite.

(　) 20. Parallelism is a rhetorical device in which identical words are used but not necessarily in identical position.

(　) 21. Syllable refers to a vowel sound either with or without a consonant or consonants in clusters.

(　) 22. Ethnical words refer to those words used in special professions.

II. Fill in the blanks.

1. Style can be defined as the _____ habit of different people or characteristic of typical social situations.
2. Pause can be divided into voiced pause and _____ pause.
3. The rising pitch is employed to show the meaning of indefiniteness, uncertainty and _____.
4. With _____ style people usually offer some background information. It is usually employed in business activities.
5. _____ is defined in the New Edition of the Oxford Concise Dictionary (1976) as "Substitution of mild or vague or roundabout expression for harsh or direct one; expression thus substituted."

6. There are two main types of sonnet forms in the English literature: one is the _____, which consists of an _____ rhyming abba abba followed by a _____ which combines two or three different rhymes; the other is the _____, organized into three _____ and one _____ that follow the pattern _____.
7. Phoneme is the smallest _____ unit in a specific language capable of semantic distinction.
8. The three factors of register are _____, tenor, and mode.
9. A sentence made up of two or more simple sentences, joined together by conjunctions or punctuations is a _____ sentence.
10. Stylistics may be defined as the study of or the investigation of _____.
11. The relationship between irony and humor is that irony is a language means while humor is an _____.
12. There are _____ main branches in phonetics.
13. To attract readers' _____ is one of the functions of English advertisements.
14. _____, wherein a specific part of something is used to refer to the whole, is usually understood as a specific kind of metonymy. Sometimes, however, people make an absolute distinction between a metonym and a _____, treating _____ as different from rather than inclusive of _____. There is a similar problem with the usage of simile and metaphor.
15. An _____ is a compressed _____, formed by the conjoining of two contrasting, contradictory or incongruous terms, as in bitter-sweet memories.
16. The falling pitch is used to show the meaning of definiteness, certainty and _____.
17. General stylistics is chiefly concerned with the investigation of the _____ features of all kinds of language use.
18. Stress, _____, pause, and voice quality are the four phonetic means in English.
19. There are different types of norms. They are: general norm, _____ norm and lexical norm. Example is _____ does not use capital letter at all and he does not use punctuation marks.

20. The fall-rise pitch is used to give people some encouragement or give people a _____.

21. _____ is a comparison (usually introduced by *like* or *as*) between two things that are generally not alike; _____ also offer figurative comparisons, but these are implied rather than introduced by *like* or *as*.

22. A _____ is a figure of speech consisting of a statement or proposition which on the face of it seems self-contradictory, absurd or contrary to established fact or practice, but which on further thinking and study may prove to be true, well-founded, and even to contain a succinct point.

23. People usually use casual style between friends, acquaintances, or insiders. Its main feature is that people usually employ ellipsis, _____ or cants with it.

24. There are three major principles of stylistics they are: _____ , _____ and _____.

25. The rise-fall pitch is employed to give people a sincere praise or to show the feeling of _____.

III. Multiple Choice.

( ) 1. *Leda and Swan* written by Yeats is relating to _____.
    A. Bible   B. Greek mythology   C. English myth   D. Fairy tale

( ) 2. What are the grammatical functions of stress?
    A. Emphasize a certain word or meaning.
    B. Distinguish words, phrases, same spelling, different meaning.
    C. Change of stress in words causes change of phonemes.
    D. Means of expressing strong emotions.

( ) 3. What are the levels of stylistic analysis?
    A. Phonological level   B. Lexical level
    C. Syntactic level   D. Discoursal level

( ) 4. Bathsheba in Thomas Hardy's novel is an allusion to _____.
    A. Bible   B. Greek mythology   C. English myth   D. Fairy tale

Chapter 16 Stylistics

(   ) 5. What figure of speech has been used in "many hands make light work"?
   A. irony   B. overstatement   C. synecdoche   D. oxymoron

(   ) 6. The smallest unit in a language that carries meaning is _____.
   A. pheme   B. morpheme   C. phone   D. word

(   ) 7. The term _____ is borrowed by stylisticians from art criticism, which distinguishes between the foreground and the background of a painting.
   A. deviation   B. prominence   C. norm   D. foregrounding

(   ) 8. What are the functions of inverted sentence?
   A. For effect
   B. For emphasis
   C. For balance
   D. For cohesion and conjunction

(   ) 9. Style is the _____ from the norm.
   A. diversion   B. deviation   C. detour   D. derivation

(   ) 10. _____ is a literary or rhetorical stylistic device that consists in repeating the same consonant sound at the beginning of several words in close succession.
   A. Consonance
   B. Assonance
   C. Alliteration
   D. Pararhyme

(   ) 11. What figure of speech has been used in "the young hunter was as strong as a lion"?
   A. metaphor   B. metonymy   C. synecdoche   D. simile

(   ) 12. Which of the following originate from Anglo-Saxon?
   A. members of the family
   B. time
   C. law
   D. science

(   ) 13. Which of the following are the types of change of meaning of English words?
   A. extension
   B. specialization
   C. degradation
   D. elevation

(   ) 14. What are the basic components of the English vocabulary?
   A. Anglo-Saxon   B. Greek   C. Latin   D. French

199

IV. Define the following terms.

stylistics	rhetorics	poetics
structural linguistics	foregrounding theory	philology
monism	register	the Prague School
style deviance	New Criticism	literary stylistics
time variant	monologue	genre
stylistics variation		

V. Answer the following questions briefly.

1. What are the general features of literary language?
2. How many types of style deviations did G. Leech mention in his study of stylistics? Please choose to explain at least 5 types of them with examples.
3. Use Grice's cooperative principle to analyze the following dialogue.

   Girl: And what film are you making at the moment?

   Albert: I'm on holiday.

   Girl: Where do you work?

   Albert: I'm freelance.
4. How to analyze dramatic texts?

VI. Fulfill the following tasks.

1. How would the following words be represented phonemically?

   (1) spun (2) kite (3) sell (4) pot (5) car

   (6) tiger (7) tank (8) length (9) cinema (10) traffic

2. Can you complete the rhyming scheme for the rest of the poem? As fits rhymes with wits it is also a b rhyme:

Of this world's theatre, in which we stay,	a
My love like the spectator idly sits	b
Beholding me that all the pageants play,	a
Disguising diversity my trouble wits	b

Sometimes I joy when glad occasion fits,   b
And mask to mirth like to a comedy;
Sooner after, when my joy to sorrow flits,
I wail and make my woes a tragedy.

Yet she, beholding me with constant eye,
Delights not in my mirth, nor rues my smart;
But, when I laugh, she mocks, and when I cry,
She laughs, and hardens evermore her heart.
What then can move her? If nor mirth nor moan,
She is no woman, but a senseless stone.

3. What different forms of sound patterning can you find in the first stanza of the poem, "Easter Wings", by George Herbert (who lived 1593–1663)?

> Lord, who createdst man in wealth and store,
> Though foolishly he lost the same,
> Decaying more and more,
> Till he became
> Most poore:
> With thee
> O let me rise
> As larks, harmoniously,
> And sing this day thy victories:
> Then shall the fall further the fight in me.

4. Can you identify the metres in the following lines? (27 is completely regular, but 28 and 29 have variations in their metre) What effect is achieved?

27 Wild Nights–Wild Nights!
   Were I with thee
   Wild Nights should be
   Our luxury!

28 He is not here; but far away

A Collection of Exercises in Linguistics

> The noise of life begins again,
> And ghastly through the drizzling rain
> On the bald street breaks the blank day.

29 Nobody heard him, the dead man,
> But still he lay moaning:
> I was much further out than you thought
> And not waving but drowning

5. The following is a poem by Fleur Adcock. Make a list of all the words that you can clearly assign to the category of nouns, verbs, adverbs and adjectives. What are the words you have left over, and how would you try to classify them?

Immigrant

> November' 63: eight months in London.
> I pause on the low bridge to watch the pelicans:
> They float swanlike, arching their white necks
> Over only slightly ruffled bundles of wings,
> Burying awkward beaks in the lake's water.
> I clench cold fist in my Marks and Spencer's jacket
> And secretly test my accent once again:
> St Jmaes's Park: St Jmaes's Park: St Jmaes's Park.

6. The passage below contains a high proportion of various types of noun phrases. How many of them can you identity, and which is the "head" noun in each one?

> A succession of hands, dry, cold, moist, reluctant or firm clasped his. Grace Willison, the middle-aged spinster, a study in grey; skin, hair, dress, stockings, all of them slightly dingy so that she looked like an old-fashioned, stiffly jointed doll neglected too long in a dusty cupboard.

7. How would you break the paragraph below into more manageable "chunks" of clauses if you had to rewrite it?

> This project is based on the language used by first generation Jamaicans who have been living in the UK since the 1950s. Given that they are first generation Jamaican as opposed to their children who may have been born

in England their speech will be explored to see whether there is a constant use of Jamaican Creole or if there are any other influences such as London Jamaican a term used by Mark Sebba which describes how young people some of whom are not of Jamaican descent use a linguistic variety which is in part similar to Jamaican Creole as well as being the English which is spoken by White London contemporaries.

8. Suggest hyponyms for the following.
   (1) The media   (2) Jewellery   (3) Soup
   (4) Fastenings for clothes   (5) Stationery
9. Suggest superordinates for the following.
   (1) Jazz   (2) Wheat   (3) Fountain pen   (4) Central heating
   (5) Igloo   (6) Dictionary   (7) Suitcase
10. The poem below by Sylvia Plath is full of explicit metaphors, and also contains some similes.

You're

Clownlike, happiest on your hands,
Feet to the stars, and moon-skulled,
Gilled like a fish. A common-sense
Thumbs-down on the dodo's mode.
Wrapped up in yourself like a spool,
Trawling your dark as owls do.
Mute as a turnip from the Fourth
Of July to All Fools' Day,
O high-riser, my little loaf.

Vague as a fog and looked for like mail.
Farther off than Australia.
Bent-backed Atlas, our travelled prawn.
Snug as a bug and at home
Like a sprat in a pickle jug.

A Collection of Exercises in Linguistics

>A creel of eels all ripples.
>
>Jumpy as a Mexican Bean.
>
>Right, like a well-done sum.
>
>A clean slate, with your own face on.

(1) Identify the metaphors, and their ground, tenor and vehicle

(2) Identify the similes (these also can be explained in terms of ground, tenor and vehicle)

11. The following extracts are taken from newspaper cuttings, which are often a rich source of figurative language. Identify the type of trope employed by each extract, and if appropriate, analyze it in terms of collocation or vehicle, tenor and ground.

    (1) Buckingham Palace has already been told the train may be axed when the trail network has been privatised.

    [Daily Mirror 2 February 1993, p.2]

    (2) Ted Dexter confessed last night that England are in a right old spin as to how they can beat India this winter.

    [Daily Mirror 2 February 1993, p.26]

    (3) Pet Rabbits put in peril by red tape on vaccine

    The pet rabbit population is at risk from the killer disease myxomatosis because the one man who supplied all of Britain's vaccine has ceased production in the face of costly new Ministry of Agriculture regulations and red tape.

    [Daily Telegraph 2 February 1993, p.1]

12. Try to retell as much of the extract from *Finnegans Wake* below in your own words as you can.

    Eins within a space and a wearywide space it was ere wohned a Mookse. The onesomeness wast alltolonely, archunisitlike, broady oval, and a Mookse he would a walking go (My hood! Cries Antony Romeo), so one grandsumer evening, after a great morning and his good supper of gammon and spittish, having flabelled his eyes, pilleoled his nostrils, vacticanated his ears and palliumed his throats, he put on his impermeable, seized his impugnable, harped on his crown and steepped out of his immobile *De Rure Albo*...

13. In the poem by Edwin Morgan, *Verses for a Christmas Card*, he creates the following words:

    Harbourmoon

    Bejeweleavening

    Restorying

    Liftlike

    Can you:

    (1) Decide to which part of speech each word belongs(e.g. Noun, verb etc.);

    (2) List other words they resemble;

    (3) Work out their morphological structure?

14. Collect a few magazine adverts and look for instances of direct address to the reader. Can you categorize these in any way—for example, according to whether they are questions or statements, or whether they restricted the scope of "you"? The think about what sort of products tend to feature direct address in their advertisements and how this is used to target readers as potential consumers.

15. Identify archaisms (grammatical, etc., as well as lexical) in the following two stanzas by Byron. To help in this, a paraphrase of the first stanza in everyday modern English. Disregarding the factor of versification, what is gained or lost by such a paraphrase?

>   Whilome in Albion's isle there dwelt a youth,
>   Who ne in virtue's ways did take delight;
>   But spent his days in riot most uncouth,
>   And vexed with mirth the drowsy ear of Night.
>   Ah, me! in sooth he was a shameless wight,
>   Sore given to revel and ungodly glee;
>   Few earthly things found favour in his sight
>   Save concubines and carnal companie,
>   And flaunting wassailers of high and low degree.

Childe Harold was he hight: — but whence his name
And lineage long, it suits me not to say;
Suffice it, that perchance they were of fame,
And had been glorious in another day:
But one sad losel soils a name for aye,
However mighty in the olden time;
Nor all that heralds rake from coffined clay,
Nor florid prose, nor honeyed lines of rhyme,
Can blazon evil deeds, or consecrate a crime.
[Childe Harold's Pilgrimage.]

16. Consider in what respects the following passages of twentieth century poetry can be interpreted as personal testimonies of the poet's struggle to 'escape from banality'. (They are discussed in R. Quirk, The Use of English, 262-3.)

So here I am, in the middle way, having had twenty years-
Twenty years largely wasted, the years of l'entre deux guerres-
Trying to use words, and every attempt
Is a wholy new start, and a different kind of failure
Because one has only learnt to get the better of words
For the thing one no longer has to say, or the way in which
One is no longer disposed to say it. And so each venture
Is a new beginning, a raid on the inarticulate,
With shabby equipment always deteriorating
In the general mess of imprecision of feeling,
Undisciplined squads of emotion.
[T. S. Eliot, East Coker]

And from the first declension of the flesh
I learnt man's tongue, to twist the shapes of thoughts
Into the stony idiom of the brain,

To shade and knit anew the patch of words
Left by the dead who, in their moonless acre,
Need no word's warmth.
[Dylan Thomes, From Love's First Fever to her Plague]

17. Discuss the nature and artistic function of phonological and formal schemes in these two poems, placing them within the total interpretation of each.

Bantams in Pin Woods

Chieftain Iffucan of Azcan in caftan
Of tan with henna hackles halt!
Damned universal cock, as if the sun
Was blackamoor to bear your blazing tail.
Fat! Fat! Fat! Fat! I am the personal.
Your world is you. I am my world.
You ten-foot poet among inchlings. Fat!
Begone! An inchling bristles in these pines,
Bristles, and points their Appalachian tangs,
And fears not portly Azan nor his hoos.
[Wallace Stevens]

This Bread I Break

This bread I break was once the oat,
This wine upon a foreign tree
Plunged in its fruit;
Man in the day or wind at night
Laid the crops low, broke the grape's joy.

Once in this wine the summer blood
Knocked in the flesh that decked the vine,
Once in this bread

> The oat was merry in the wind;
> Man broke the sun, pulled the wind down.
> This flesh you break, this blood you let
> Make desolation in the vein,
> Were oat and grape
> Born of the sensual root and sap;
> My wine you drink, my bread you snap.
> [Dylan Thomes]

18. Indicate what kind of figures of speech is used in the following examples.

    (1) —Where have you been for the last four years?

    —At college taking medicine.

    —And did you get well?

    (2) Life is but a brief candle.

    (3) From the cradle to the grave

    (4) Many hands make light work.

    (5) She's as old as a mountain.

    (6) —What weather do the mice dislike?

    —When it rains cats and dogs.

    (7) He is a fool. He never knows where his personal interest lies. His whole heart is concerned about the interest of other people.

    (8) Belinda smiled, and all the world was gay.

    (9) The drunkard loves his bottle better than his wife.

    (10) —Why are parliamentary reports called "blue books"?

    —Because they are never red.

    (11) The young hunter was as strong as a lion.

    (12) —What starts with T, ends with T, and is full of T?

    —Teapot.

    —And did you get well?

    (13) A victorious defeat

    (14) My love is a red, red rose.

Appendixes

Appendix 1
Keys to the Exercises

Chapter 1 Language and Linguistics

I.
1-5 TTTTT   6-10 TFFFT   11-15 FTFTF   16-20 TTTTF
21-25 TFFTF   26-30 FFFFT   31-34 TFFF

II.
1. genetic 2. sound 3. abstract 4. productive 5. knowledge 6. system
7. applied 8. syntax 9. Duality 10. arbitrary 11. arbitrary 12. Pragmatics
13. scientific

III.
1-5 ACDDD   6-10 BBBCC   11-15 BDDDC   16-20 BBACA
21-25 DCCCA   26-30 AADAD   31-35 CACAA   36-40 DCBCA
41-45 DABDD   46-50 AAABA

VI.
1. arbitrariness, duality, productivity, displacement, stimulus-freedom, discreteness, interchangeability 2. human 3. sound, meaning 4. voiced, voiceless, voiced
5. Assimilation 6. Symbolic 7. manner, place 8. Phonetics, phonology
9. Arbitrariness 10. Phatic 11. Descriptive, creative 12. evolutionary
13. Displacement 14. descriptive 15. productive 16. descriptive 17. allophones
18. minimal pair 19. minimal 20. diphthongs 21. synchronic 22. morpheme
23. obstruction 24. Phoneme 25. bilabial 26. position 27. syllable stress, tone

28. Articulatory 29. speech 30. bilabial 31. complementary 32. tongue
33. nasal 34. diachronic 35. Langue 36. nucleus, vowel 37. allophone
38. stops 39. complementary 40. bilabial 41. General linguistics 42. velar
43. Indo-European 44. diachronic 45. scientific

Chapter 2 Phonetics and Phonology

I.
1-5 FFFTF   6-10 FFTFT   11-15 TFTTT   16-20 FTTTT   21-25 FTFFT
26-30 FFTFF   31-35 FTFTF   36-40 TTFTT

II.
1-5 CABAA   6-10 DCCDD   11-15 DCBAA   16-20 CACBD   21-25 BDDDA

Chapter 3 Morphology

I.
1-5 FTFTF   6-10 TFTTT   11-15 TTTTT   16-20 TTFTT   21-24 FTTT

II.
1. Morpheme   2. suffix   3. Derivative   4. morphological   5. stem
6. grammatical   7. Bound   8. derivative   9. Compounding   10. derivation

III.
1-5 DABDD   6-10 CDCDC   11-15 BABCC

V.
1. expression, content   2. USA, IMF   3. Acronyms   4. Bound
5. grammatical   6. Morpheme   7. phoneme, morpheme

Chapter 4 Semantics

I.
1-5 FFTFT   6-10 TFTTT   11-15 TFTFF   16-20 FTFFF
21-25 TTTFT   26-29 FTFT

II.
1. Semantics 2. direct   3. Reference   4. synonyms   5. homophones

6. Relational   7. Componential   8. selectional   9. argument   10. naming
III.
1-5 BACCA   6-10 ABDDB   11-15 CBDBC   16-20 CACDB

Chapter 5 Syntax

I.
1-5 FTFTT   6-10 TTFFT   11-15 FTTTF   16-20 TFTTF   21-23 TTT
II.
1. simple   2. sentence   3. subject   4. predicate   5. complex
6. embedded   7. open   8. Adjacency   9. Parameters   10. case
III.
1-5 BCADD   6-10 AACDD

Chapter 6 Pragmatics

I.
1-5 FFTTF   6-10 FFFFT   11-15 TFFFT   16-20 FTTFF
21-25 FTFFT   26-29 TTFF
II.
1. Pragmatics   2. semantics   3. context   4. utterance   5. abstract
6. Constatives   7. Performatives   8. locutionary   9. illocutionary   10. commissive
11. expressive   12. quantity   13. meaning   14. deixis   15. quality
16. performative   17. felicity
III.
1-5 ACDBC   6-10 ACCBB   11-12 AD
IV.
pragmatics: Pragmatics can be defined as the study of how speakers of a language use sentences to effect successful communication.

context: Generally speaking, it consists of the knowledge that is shared by the speaker and the hearer. The shared knowledge is of two types: the knowledge of the language they use, and the knowledge about the world, including the general knowledge about the world and the specific knowledge about the situation in which linguistic communication is taking place.

utterance meaning: The meaning of an utterance is concrete, and context-dependent. Utterance is based on sentence meaning; it is realization of the abstract meaning of a sentence in a real situation of communication, or simply in a context.

sentence meaning: The meaning of a sentence is often considered as the abstract, intrinsic property of the sentence itself in terms of a predication.

constative: Constatives were statements that either state or describe, and were verifiable.

performative: Performatives, on the other hand, were sentences that did not state a fact or describe a state, and were not verifiable. Their function is to perform a particular speech act.

locutionary act: A locutionary act is the act of uttering words, phrases, clauses. It is the act of conveying literal meaning by means of syntax, lexicon and phonology.

illocutionary act: An illocutionary act is the act of expressing the speaker's intention; it is the act performed in saying something.

perlocutionary act: A perlocutionary act is the act performed by or resulting from saying something; it is the consequence of, or the change brought about by the utterance; it is the act performed by saying something.

cooperative principle: It is a principle advanced by Paul Grice. It is a principle that guides our conversational behaviors. The content is: Make your conversational contribution such as is required at the stage at which it occurs by the accepted purpose or the talk exchange in which you are engaged.

speech act theory: A theory proposed by J. L. Austin and has been developed by J. R. Searle, asserting that language is not only used to inform or to describe things, it is often used to "do things", to perform acts.

deixis: A particular way in which the interpretation of certain linguistic expressions is dependent on the context they are produced or interpreted.

reference: the act by which a speaker or writer uses language to enable a hearer or reader to identify something.

anaphora: the process where a word or phrase refers back to another word or phrase which was used earlier in a text or conversation.

presupposition: an unstated assumption underlying an utterance in a given context and being held true of the conventional background by the speaker.

indirect speech act: an act performing the communicative functions that are usually associated with another structural form.

politeness principle: the principle put forth by Leech to rescue the CP in the sense that politeness as a strategy can account for why people are often so indirect in conveying what they mean.

V.

1. How are semantics and pragmatics different from each other?

Traditional semantics studied meaning, but the meaning of language was considered as something intrinsic, and inherent, i.e. a property attached to language itself. Therefore, meanings of words, meanings of sentences were all studied in an isolated manner, detached from the context in which they were used. Pragmatics studies meaning not in isolation, but in context. The essential distinction between semantics and pragmatics is whether the context of use is considered in the study of meaning. If it is not considered, the study is restricted to the area of traditional semantics; if it is considered, the study is being carried out in the area of pragmatics.

2. How does a sentence differ from an utterance?

A sentence is a grammatical concept. It usually consists of a subject and predicate. An utterance is the unit of communication. It is the smallest linguistic unit that has a communicative value. If we regard a sentence as what people actually utter in the course of communication, it becomes an utterance. Whether "Mary is beautiful." is a sentence or an utterance depends on how we look at it. If we regard it as a grammatical unit or a self-contained unit in isolation, then it is a sentence. If we look at it as something uttered in a certain situation with a certain purpose, then it is an utterance. Most utterances take the form of complete sentences, but some utterances are not, and some cannot even be restored to complete sentences.

3. How does a sentence meaning differ from an utterance meaning?

A sentence meaning is often considered as the intrinsic property of the sentence itself in terms of a predication. It is abstract and independent of context. The meaning of an utterance is concrete, and context-dependent. The utterance meaning is based on sentence meaning; it is realization of the abstract meaning of a sentence in a real situation of communication, or simply in a context. For example, "There is a dog at the door." The speaker could utter it as a matter-of-fact statement, telling the hearer that the dog is at the door. The speaker could use it as a warning, asking the hearer not to approach the door. There are other possibilities, too. So, the understanding of the utterance meaning of "There is a dog at the door" depends on the context in which it is uttered and the purpose for which the speaker utters it.

4. Discuss in detail the locutionary act, illocutionary act and perlocutionary act.

A locutionary act is the act of uttering words, phrases, clauses. It is the act of conveying literal meaning by means of syntax, lexicon and phonology. An illocutionary act is the act of expressing the speaker's intention; it is the act performed in saying something. A perlocutionary act is the act performed by or resulting from saying something; it is the consequence of, or the change brought about by the utterance; it is the act performed by saying something. For example:

You have left the door wide open.

The locutionary act performed by the speaker is that he has uttered all the words "you" "have" "door" "left" "open" etc. and expressed what the word literally mean.

The illocutionary act performed by the speaker is that by making such an utterance, he has expressed his intention of asking the hearer to close the door.

The perlocutionary act refers to the effect of the utterance. If the hearer understands that the speaker intends him to close the door and closes the door, the speaker has successfully brought about the change in the real world he has intended to; then the perlocutiohary act is successfully performed.

5. Searle classified illocutionary act into five categories. Discuss each of them in detail with examples.

1) **representatives:** representatives are used to state, to describe, to report,

etc. The illocutionary point of the representatives is to commit the speaker to something's being the case, to the truth of what has been said. For example:

(I swear) I have never seen the man before.

(I state) the earth is a globe.

2) directives: Directives are attempts by the speaker to get the hearer to do something. Inviting, suggesting, requesting, advising, warning, threatening, ordering are all specific instances of this class. For example:

Open the window!

3) commissives: Commissives are those illocutionary acts whose point is to commit the speaker to some future course of action. When the speaker is speaking, he puts himself under obligation. For example:

I promise to come.

I will bring you the book tomorrow without fail.

4) expressives: The illocutionary point of expressives is to express the psychological state specified in the utterance. The speaker is expressing his feelings or attitude towards an existing state of affairs, e.g. apologizing, thanking, congratulating. For example:

I'm sorry for the mess I have made.

5) declarations: Declarations have the characteristic that the successful performance of such an act brings about the correspondence between what is said and reality. For example:

I now declare the meeting open.

6. What are the four maxims under the cooperative principle?

The maxim of quantity

(1) Make your contribution as informative as required (for the current purpose of the exchange).

(2) Do not make your contribution more informative than is required.

The maxim of quality

(1) Do not say what you believe to be false.

(2) Do not say that for which you lack adequate evidence.

A Collection of Exercises in Linguistics

The maxim of relation

Be relevant.

The maxim of manner

(1) Avoid obscurity of expression.

(2) Avoid ambiguity.

(3) Be brief (avoid unnecessary prolixity) .

(4) Be orderly.

7. How does the flouting of the maxims give rise to conversational implicatures?

A: Do you know where Mr. Smith lives?

B: Somewhere in the southern suburbs of the city.

This is said when both A and B know that B does know Mr. Smith's address. Thus B does not give enough information that is required, and he has flouted the maxim of quantity. Therefore, such conversational implicature as "I do not wish to tell you where Mr. Smith lives" is produced.

A: Would you like to come to our party tonight?

B: I'm afraid I'm not feeling so well today.

This is said when both A and B know that B is not having any health problem that will prevent him from going to a party. Thus B is saying something that he himself knows to be false and he is violating the maxim of quality. The conversational implicature "I do not want to go to your party tonight" is then produced.

A: The hostess is an awful bore. Don't you think?

B: The roses in the garden are beautiful, aren't they?

This is said when both A and B know that it is entirely possible for B to make a comment on the hostess. Thus B is saying something irrelevant to what A has just said, and he has flouted the maxim of relation. The conversational implicature "I don't wish to talk about the hostess in such a rude manner" is produced.

A: Shall we get something for the kids?

B: Yes. But I veto I - C - E - C - R - E - A - M.

This is said when both A and B know that B has no difficulty in pronouncing the word "ice-cream". Thus B has flouted the maxim of manner. The conversational implicature "I don't want the kids to know we are talking about ice-cream" is then produced.

Chapter 7   Discourse Analysis

I.

1-5 FFTTT   6-10 TTFTT

II.

1-5 CAADC   6-9 CABC

III.

sociolect: the linguistic variety used by people belonging to a particular social class.

bilingualism: the situation where at least two languages are used side by side by an individual or by a group of speakers, with each having a different role to play.

the Whorf-Sapir hypothesis: the suggestion that different languages carve the world up in different ways, and that as a result their speakers think about it differently.

a speech community: a community the members of which have or believe they have at least one common variety of language.

performatives: sentences that do not describe things and cannot be said to be true or false.

registers: varieties of language that are related to use.

a proposition: what is expressed by a declarative sentence when that sentence is uttered to make a statement.

an utterance: a piece of language actually used in a particular context.

constatives: sentences which describe or state something; they are either true or false.

utterance meaning: something conveyed by a sentence in a context other than its literal meaning.

Chapter 8 Teaching Methodologies and Testing

I.

1-5 BCDBC   6-10 ACDAC   11-15 DBBCD   16-20 DAAAD

21-25 ADBBC   26-30 DABDA   31-35 ABBDC   36-37 DB

II.

3.

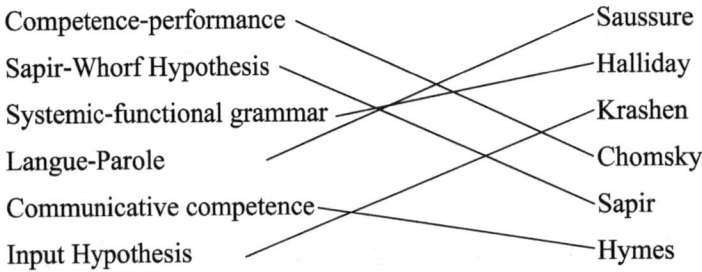

Chapter 9 Language Acquisition

I.

1-5 FTFFF   6-10 FFFFT   11-15 TTTFT   16-20 TTTFFT

21-25 TFTTF   26-30 TFFFF   31-35 TFTTF   36-39 TTFT

II.

1. transfer   2. target   3. interlanguage   4. Instrumental, integrative   5. puberty   6. Acquisition   7. Constrative   8. acquisition   9. nativist   10. motherese, baby talk   11. Behavioristic   12. holophrastic   13. acquire   14. pidgin, creole   15. telegraphic

III.

1-5 ADDCC   6-10 AADDB   11-15 DACDA   16-20 BADBC

21-25 BCDDB   26-29 DCAA

IV.

acquisition & learning

　　The term "acquisition" is used to refer to picking up a second language through exposure, whereas the term "learning" is used to refer to the conscious study of a second language. Now most of the researchers use them interchangeably, irrespective of whether conscious or unconscious processes are involved.

incidental learning

While reading for pleasure a reader does not bother to look up a new word in a dictionary, but a few pages later realizes what that word means, then incidental learning is said to have taken place.

intentional learning

If a student is instructed to read a text and find out the meanings of unknown words, then it becomes an intentional learning activity.

language

Language is a system of arbitrary vocal symbols used for human communication. That is to say, language is systematic (rule-governed), symbolic and social.

error analysis

Error analysis aims to 1) find out how well the learner knows a second language, 2) find out how the learner learns a second language, 3) obtain information on common difficulties in second language learning, and to 4) serve as an aid in teaching or in the preparation and compilation of teaching materials (Corder, 1981). It is a methodology of describing Second Language Learners' language systems.

interlanguage

It refers to the language that the L2 learner produced. The language produced by the learner is a system in its own right. The language is a dynamic system, evolving over time.

Monitor Model

    a) The Acquisition-Learning Hypothesis

    b) The Monitor Hypothesis

    c) The Natural Hypothesis

    d) The Input Hypothesis

    e) The Affective Filter Hypothesis

affective filter hypothesis

The hypothesis is based on the theory of an affective filter, which states that successful second language acquisition depends on the learner's feelings. Negative attitudes (including a lack of motivation or self-confidence and anxiety) are said to act as a filter, preventing the learner from making use of INPUT, and thus hindering success in language learning.

Universal Grammar

The language faculty built into the human mind consisting of principles and parameters. This is the universal grammar theory associated with Noam Chomsky. Universal Grammar sees the knowledge of grammar in the mind as having two components: "principles" that all languages have in common and "parameters" on which they vary.

fossilization

It refers to the phenomenon in which second language learners often stop learning even though they might be far short of native-like competence. The term is also used for specific linguistic structures that remain incorrect for lengthy periods of time in spite of plentiful input.

Shumann's Acculturation Model

This model of second language acquisition was formulated by Schumann (1978), and applies to the natural context of second language acquisition where a second language is acquired without any instruction in the environment. Schumann defines acculturation as the process of becoming adapted to a new culture or rather, the social and psychological integration of the learner with the target language group.

V.

1. Summarize the individual differences in second language acquisition.

The individual differences include personal interests, motivation, learning style, learning aptitude, learning strategies, etc.

2. What are the differences of error analysis from contrastive analysis?

Contrastive analysis stresses the interfering effects of a first language on second language learning and claims that most errors come from interference of the first language. (Corder, 1967). However, such a narrow view of interference ignores the intralingual effects of language learning among other factors. Error analysis is the method to deal with intralingual factors in learners' language (Corder, 1981). It is a methodology of describing Second Language Learners' language systems.

Error analysis is a type of bilingual comparison, a comparison between learners' interlanguage and a target language, while contrastive analysis between languages (native language and target language).

3. What are the beneficial views obtained from the studies on children's L1 acquisition?

a) Children's language acquisition goes through several stages;

b) These stages are very similar across children for a given language, although the rate at which individual children progress through them is highly variable;

c) These stages are similar across languages;

d) Child language is rule-governed and systematic, and the rules created by the child do not necessarily correspond to adult ones;

e) Children are resistant to correction;

f) Children's mental capacity limits the number of rules they can apply at any one time, and they will revert to earlier hypotheses when two or more rules compete.

5. What role does UG play in SLA?

Three possibilities:

a) UG operates in the same way for L2 as it does for L1.

b) The learner's core grammar is fixed and UG is no longer available to the L2 learner, particularly not to the adult learner.

c) UG is partly available but it is only one factor in the acquisition of L2. There are other factors and they may interfere with the UG influence.

6. What are classifications of communication strategies?

Faerch and Kasper characterize CSs in the light of learners' attempts at governing two different behaviors and their taxonomies are achievement and reduction strategies, and they are based on the psycholinguistics.

Achievement Strategies:

Paraphrase

Approximation

Word coinage

Circumlocution

Conscious Transfer

Literal translation

Language switch (borrowing)

Mime

Use body language and gestures to make communication open

Appeal for assistance

Reduction Strategies:

Message abandonment (topic shift): Ask a student to answer the question: How old are you ? She must utter two or three sentences to answer the question, but she mustn't tell her age.

Topic avoidance(Silence)

13. What are learning strategies? Give examples.

Intentional behaviour and thoughts that learners make use of during learning in order to better help them understand, learn or remember new information.

Learning strategies are classified into:

a) meta-cognitive strategies

b) cognitive strategies

c) socio-affective strategies

20. What are the factors influencing the success of SLA?

Cognitive factors:

a) Intelligence

b) Language aptitude

c) Language learning strategies

Affective factors:

a) Language attitudes

b) Motivation

22. What are the differences between the Behaviorist learning model and that of Mentalist?

Behaviorist learning model claims that children acquired the L1 by trying to imitate utterances produced by people around them and by receiving negative or positive reinforcement of their attempts to do so. Language acquisition, therefore, was considered to be environmentally determined.

Chapter 10   Cognitive Linguistics

I.

1-3 TTT

II.

cognitive linguistics: Cognitive linguistics is an enterprise or an approach to the study of language and the mind rather than a single articulated theoretical framework. It is informed by two overarching principles or commitments: the generalization commitment and the cognitive commitment. The two best developed sub-branches of cognitive linguistics are cognitive semantics and cognitive approaches to grammar.

cognitive grammar: Cognitive Grammar attempts to model the cognitive mechanisms and principles that motivate and license the formation and use of linguistic units of varying degrees of complexity.

cognitive semantics: The area of study known as cognitive semantics is concerned with investigating the relationship between experience, the conceptual system and the semantic structure encoded by language.

Cognitive semantics represents an approach rather than a single articulated theory. There are four guiding principles of cognitive semantics that characterise the approach. Some examples of theories in cognitive semantics include Blending Theory, Conceptual Metaphor Theory, Frame Semantics, Mental Spaces Theory, LCCM Theory, Principled Polysemy and approaches to linguistic semantics such as cognitive lexical semantics and encyclopaedic semantics (Evans, 2007: 26-27).

prototype: A relatively abstract mental representation that assembles the key attributes or features that best represent instances of a given category. Accordingly, the prototype is viewed as a schematic representation of the most salient or central characteristics associated with members of the category in question. According to Prototype Theory, the prototype provides structure to and serves to organise a given category, a phenomenon known as prototype structure. An important consequence of this is that categories exhibit typicality effects (Evans, 2007: 175).

grammaticalisation: The process whereby lexical or content words acquire grammatical functions or existing grammatical units acquire further grammatical functions. Grammaticalisation has received a great deal of attention within cognitive linguistics. This is because grammaticalisation is characterised by interlaced changes in the form and meaning of a given construction and can therefore be seen as a process that is essentially grounded in meaning. Furthermore, cognitive linguists argue that semantic change in grammaticalisation is a function of language use and thus is a usage-based phenomenon (Evans, 2007: 97).

Chapter 11   Language and Culture

I.
1-5 TTTFF   6-10 TTFFT   11-15 FTTFF   16-20 TTFTF   21-25 TTTFF
26-30 FFTTT   31-35 FFFTT   36-39 FTFT

II.
1. bilingualism   2. Sapir-Whorf   3. determinism   4. Acculturation
5. speech   6. relativity   7. acculturation

III.
1. evolved   2. greetings   3. medium   4. sanitation engineer   5. lie
6. concentration camps   7. intimate, personal, social, public   8. shame culture
9. language users, settings, topics   10. harmony   11. connotative   12. good and evil   13. social status or roles   14. information   15. I'm terribly sorry
16. wrong/inappropriate   17. individualism   18. Group interest, duty and loyalty, harmony, hierarchy, or modesty 任选其二   19. arbitrary vocal   20. Euphemisms
21. community   22. language   23. shared, learned, dynamic, symbolic, integrated
24. nodding, bowing, hat-off, smiling 任选其二   25. Would you like something to drink

IV.

1-5 CACCD   6-10 ADCDD   11-15 CDDAB   16-20 DBDCD

21-25 DCABA   26-30 ACDCD   31-35 AAABD

VI.

1. What is culture?

Broadly speaking, it means the total way of life of a people, including the patterns of belief, customs, objects, institutions, techniques, and language. In a narrow sense, it refers to local or specific practice, beliefs or customs.

21. What's the relationship between language and culture?

    a) Language is part of culture.

    b) Language is the carrier and container of culture.

    c) Language is influenced and shaped by culture.

    d) Language also exerts its influence on culture.

33. How to understand cultural Iceberg?

Key 1: Like an iceberg what we can see about culture is just the tip of the iceberg; the majority of it is intangible, beyond sight. And the part of culture that is visible is only a small part of a much bigger whole. It is said nine-tenth of culture is below the surface.

Key 2: Just as an iceberg which has a visible section above the waterline and a larger invisible section below the waterline, culture has some aspects that are observable and others that can only be suspected and imagined. Also like an iceberg, the part of culture that is visible is only a small part of a much bigger whole. It is said nine-tenth of culture is below the surface.

Chapter 12 Sociolinguistics

I.

1-5 TFTFF   6-10 TFFFF   11-15 FTFTF   16-20 FTTTT   21-25 TFFTF

26-30 FTFTT   31-35 TFFTT   36-40 TFTTF   41-45 TTTTF   46-50 TTTTF

51-55 FFFTF   56-60 FFFTF   61-65 FFTFF   66 T

II.
1. vernacular 2. gender 3. protolanguage 4. bilingualism 5. pidgin
6. Indio-European 7. sociolects 8. register 9. linguistic 10. society
11. community 12. variety 13. dialectal 14. speech 15. Register, idiolect
16. Sociolinguistics 17. speech community 18. inflectional 19. social
20. dialect 21. Bilingualism 22. superposedly 23. stylistic 24. synchronic
25. official 26. planning 27. euphemism 28. negative 29. geographically
30. formal 31. Idiolect 32. creole

III.
1-5 BCBDC   6-10 ACDCB   11-15 DAACC   16-20 ADCAA
21-25 ADADB   26-30 BCCAC   31 C

IV.

sociolinguistics: Sociolinguistics is the study of language in social contexts.

speech community: The social group isolated for any given study is called the speech community or a speech community is a group of people who form a community and share the same language or a particular variety of language. The important characteristic of a speech community is that the members of the group must, in some reasonable way, interact linguistically with other members of the community. They may share closely related language varieties, as well as attitudes toward linguistic norms.

speech variety: Speech variety, also known as language variety, refers to any distinguishable form of speech used by a speaker or group of speakers. The distinctive characteristics of a speech variety may be lexical, phonological, morphological, syntactic, or a combination of linguistic features.

language planning: language standardization is known as language planning. This means that certain authorities, such as the government or government agency of a country, choose a particular speech variety and spread the use of it, including its pronunciation and spelling systems, across regional boundaries.

idiolect: An idiolect is a personal dialect of an individual speaker that combines aspects of all the elements regarding regional, social, and stylistic variation, in one form or another. In a narrower sense, what makes up one's idiolect includes also such factors as voice quality, pitch and speech rhythm, which all contribute to the identifying features in an individual's speech.

standard language: The standard language is a superposed, socially prestigious dialect of language. It is the language employed by the government and the judiciary system, used by the mass media, and taught in educational institutions, including school settings where the language is taught as a foreign or second language.

nonstandard language: Language varieties other than the standard are called nonstandard languages.

lingua franca: A lingua franca is a variety of language that serves as a medium of communication among groups of people for diverse linguistic backgrounds.

pidgin: A pidgin is a variety of language that is generally used by native speakers of other languages as a medium of communication.

creole: A creole language is originally a pidgin that has become established as a native language in some speech community.

diglossia: Diglossia usually describes a situation in which two very different varieties of language co-exist in a speech community, each with a distinct range of purely social function and appropriate for certain situations.

bilingualism: Bilingualism refers to a linguistic situation in which two standard languages are used either by an individual or by a group of speakers, such as the inhabitants of a particular region or a nation.

ethnic dialect: Within a society, speech variation may come about because of different ethnic backgrounds. An ethnic language variety is a social dialect of a language, often cutting across regional differences. An ethnic dialect is spoken mainly by a less privileged population that has experienced some form of social isolation, such as racial discrimination or segregation.

sociolect: Social dialects, or sociolects, are varieties of language used by people belonging to particular social classes.

register: Registers are language varieties which are appropriate for use in particular speech situations, in contrast to language varieties that are associated with the social or regional grouping of their customary users. Format reason, registers are also known as situational dialects.

slang: Slang is a casual use of language that consists of expressive but non-standard vocabulary, typically of arbitrary, flashy and often ephemeral coinages and figures of speech characterized by spontaneity and sometimes by raciness.

euphemism: A euphemism, then, is a mild, indirect or less offensive word or expression substituted when the speaker or writer fears more direct wording might be harsh, unpleasantly direct, or offensive.

V.

1. Discuss with examples that the speech of women may differ from the speech of men.

In normal situations, female speakers tend to use more prestigious forms than their male counterparts with the same general social background. For example, standard English forms such as "I did it" and "he isn't" can be found more often in the speech of females, while the more colloquial "I done it" and "he ain't" occur more frequently in the speech of males.

Another feature often associated with so-called women's language is politeness. Usually, tough and rough speeches have connotations of masculinity and are not considered to be desirable feminine qualities. In general, men's language is more straightforward, less polite, and more direct, and women's language is more indirect, less blunt, and more circumlocutory.

This phenomenon of sex-preferential differentiation is also reflected in the relative frequency with which males and females use the same lexical items. For example, certain words that are closely associated with women may sound typically feminine as a result of that association. For example, some English adjectives like "lovely" "nice" "darling" and "cute" occur more often in female speeches and therefore cause feminine association. Females have also been shown to possess a greater variety of specific color terms than males, in spite of the fact that men do not necessarily possess less acute color perception than women. On the other hand, males have the reputation of possessing a larger vocabulary in traditionally male-dominated domains such as sports, hunting and the military.

A request in English such as "Close the door when you leave" can be phrased in a number of ways ranging from a harsh command to a very polite request:

a. Close the door when you leave.
b. Please close the door when you leave.
c. Would you please close the door when you leave?
d. Could you close the door when you leave?

Although the above options are all available to both men and women, it is usually the more polite forms that are selected by female speakers. In general, females are found to use more questions than declarative statements in comparison with males.

11. What is a linguistic taboo? What effect does it have on our use of language?

A linguistic taboo refers to a word or expression that is prohibited by the "polite" society from general use. Obscene, profane, and swear words are all taboo words that are to be avoided entirely, or at least avoided in mixed company.

In sociolinguistics, a linguistic taboo denotes any prohibition on the use of particular lexical items to refer to objects or acts. As language use is contextualized in particular social settings, linguistic taboo originates from social taboo. When an act is taboo, reference to this act may also become taboo. Taboo words and expressions reflect the particular social customs and views of a particular culture.

As linguistic taboo reflects social taboo, certain words are more likely to be avoided, for examples, the words related to sex, sex organs and excrement in many cultures. The avoidance of using taboo language mirrors social attitudes, emotions and value judgments, and has no linguistic basis.

The avoidance of using taboo language has led to the creation of euphemisms. A euphemism is a mild, indirect or less offensive word or expression substituted when the speaker or writer fears more direct wording might be harsh, unpleasantly direct, or offensive. For example, we say "portly" instead of "fat".

In many cultures, people avoid using direct words that pertain to death or dying because it is the subject that everyone fears and is unpleasant to talk about. In the

English-speaking world, for example, people do not "die", but "pass away".

23. Discuss with examples some of the linguistic differences between Standard English and Black English.

One of the most prominent phonological characteristics of Black English is the frequent simplification of consonant clusters at the end of words when one of the two consonants is an alveolar /t/, /d/, /s/, or /z/. The application of this simplification rule may delete the past - tense morpheme, so "past" and "passed" are both pronounced like "pass."

Another salient characteristic of Black English phonological system concerns the deletion of some word-final stop consonants in words like "side" and "borrowed." Speakers of Black English frequently delete these word-final stops, pronouncing "side" like "sigh" and "borrowed" like "borrow."

One prominent syntactic feature is the frequent absence of various forms of the copula "be" in Black English, which are required of Standard English. Compare the following expressions in Black English and Standard English:

Black English	Standard English
They mine.	They' re mine.
You crazy.	You're crazy.

Another distinctive syntactic feature of Black English is the systematic use of the expression "it is" where Standard English uses "there is" in the sense of "there exists":

Is it a Mr. Johnson in this office?

Another aspect of Black English is the use of double negation constructions. Whenever the verb is negated, the indefinite pronouns "something" "somebody", and "some" become the negative indefinites "nothing" "nobody", and "none", for example:

He don't know nothing. (He doesn't know anything.)

Chapter 13 Psycholinguistics

I.

1-5 TTFTT   6-10 TTFTT   11-15 FTTTF   16-20 FFFTT   21-24 FTFT

II.
1-5 AADBA   6-10 BAAAB   11-15 BCABA   16-20 ACCAA
21-25 DABAC   26-30 BBBCB   31-35 ADCBB   36-40 CDCCA
41-45 CBDAA   46-50 DAAAA   51-55 ADBAA   56-60 ABBBA   61-63 CAC

Chapter 14   Neurolinguistics

I.
1-5 TFFTT   6-10 FTTTT   11-15 TFFTT   16-19 TTFT
II.
1. hemispheres   2. gyrus   3. lateralization   4. dichotic   5. nativist   6. Cerebral
7. frontal lobe   8. left   9. brain and language   10. lateralization
III.
1-5 DACBD   6-10 CCCAC   11-14 AABB

Chapter 15   Corpus Linguistics

I.
答案从略。
II.
答案从略。

Chapter 16   Stylistics

I.
1-5 TFTTT   5-10 TTFTF   11-15 FFFFF   16-20 FFFTF   21-22 TT
II.
1. linguistic   2. silent   3. incompleteness   4. consultative   5. Euphemism
6. Italian/Petrarchan sonnet, octave, sestet, English sonnet, quatrains, closing couplet, abab cdcd efef gg   7. sound   8. field   9. compound   10. style   11. effect
12. three   13. attention   14. Synecdoche, synecdoche, synecdoche, metonymy
15. oxymoron, expression   16. completeness   17. linguistic   18. intonation
19. authorian, E. E. Cummings   20. warning   21. Simile, metaphors   22. paradox

A Collection of Exercises in Linguistics

23. slangs   24. Foregrounding, Norm, Deviation   25. shock

III.

1. B   2. ABCD   3. ABCD   4. A   5. C   6. B   7. D   8. BCD   9. B   10. C   11. D   12. AB   13. ABCD   14. ACD

VI.

18. Indicate what kind of figures of speech is used in the following examples.

(1) pun   (2) metaphor   (3) metonymy   (4) synecdoche   (5) hyperbole
(6) pun   (7) irony   (8) overstatement/hyperbole   (9) metonymy   (10) pun
(11) simile   (12) pun   (13) oxymoron   (14) metaphor

Appendix 2
A Model Test of Linguistics

I. Multiple Choice. (20 points)

Mark the choice that can best complete the statement.

1. The phenomenon that words having different meanings have the same form is called _____.
   A. polysemy　　　　　　　　　B. hyponymy
   C. antonymy　　　　　　　　　D. homonymy

2. The level of syntactic representation that exists before movement takes place is commonly termed the _____.
   A. phrase structure　　　　　　B. surface structure
   C. syntactic structure　　　　　D. deep structure

3. In first language acquisition children usually _____ grammatical rules from the linguistic information they hear.
   A. use　　　　　　　　　　　　B. accept
   C. generalize　　　　　　　　　D. reconstruct

4. Basically all the following categories except _____ are always missing in the children's telegraphic speech stage.
   A. the copula verb "be"　　　　B. inflectional morphemes
   C. function words　　　　　　　D. content words

5. "Interviewer" and "interviewee" are a pair of _____ opposites.
   A. complementary　　B. gradable　　C. complete　　D. relational

6. "We vowed to fight on until all our demands were met" is a sentence _____.
   A. coordinate　　　B. complex　　C. compound　　D. simple

7. When a _____ comes to be adopted by a population as its primary language and children learn it as their first language, it becomes _____.

A. creole, pidgin   B. pidgin, creole
C. regional dialect, lingua franca   D. lingua franca, regional dialect

8. "How fast did he drive when he ran the red light?" _____ "He ran the red light."
A. entails   B. contradicts
C. presupposes   D. includes

9. When a child uses "mummy" to refer to any woman, most probably his "mummy" means _____.
A. + Human   B. + Human + Adult
C. + Human + Adult – Male   D. + Human + Adult – Male + Parent

10. "Sweets" and "candy" are used respectively in Britain in and America, but refer to the same thing. The words are _____ synonyms.
A. collocational   B. dialectal
C. complete   D. stylistic

II. Define the Following Terms. (10 points)

1. adjacency pairs
2. conversational implicatures
3. derivational affix
4. universal grammar
5. perlocutionary act

III. Answer the Following Questions. (40 points)

1. Sociolinguistics aims to provide models of the communicative competence of members of a speech community. Discuss the factors which a sociolinguist must consider in attempting to achieve this aims.

2. What is the difference between linguistic competence and communicative competence?

3. What are "indirect speech acts"? Show how the use of indirect speech act can signal politeness and deference in English or Chinese.

4. Apply the following concepts to language teaching and/or learning.

input and interaction

IV. Essay Questions. (30 points)

1. How much does our language influence the way we think? How deeply do language and culture interpenetrate and influence one another? These questions about language have fascinated thinkers throughout the ages. For example, Johann Gottfried Herder and Wilhelm von Humboldt in the German Romantic tradition regarded language as a prisma or grid spread over things in the world so that each language reflects a different worldview. Write a short essay to explain your position on this view.

2. Read the following passages and develop the following topics into an essay about 200 words.

The linguistic theory is concerned primarily with an ideal speaker-learner, in a completely homogeneous speech-community, who knows its language perfectly and is unaffected by such grammatically irrelevant conditions as memory limitations, distractions, shifts of attention and interest, and errors (random or characteristic) in applying his knowledge of the language in actual performance... (Noam Chomsky: *Aspects of the Theory of Syntax* ,1965)

The engagement of language in social life has a positive, productive aspect. There are rules of use without which the rules of grammar would be useless. Just as rules of syntax can control aspects of phonology, and just as semantic rules perhaps control aspects of syntax, so rules of speech acts enter as a controlling factor for linguistic form as a whole. (D. H. Hymes: "On communicative competence" 1972)

In the first passage, Chomsky presents the orthodox doctrine that is criticized by Hymes in the next. What reasons do you think are there for saying that the idealization makes it theoretically possible or impossible to do any linguistic analysis possible at all? "There are rules of use without which the rules of grammar would be useless." What do you think Hymes has in mind here? Can you think of examples of such "rules of use"?

Appendix 3
A Qualifying Exam for MA Prospects

第一部分：语言学（50分）

I. Complete each of the following statements. (5 points/1 point for each)

1. _____ refers to the role language plays in communication(e.g. to express ideas, attitudes) or in particular social situations(e.g. religious, legal).
2. _____ is said of the study of development of language and languages over time.
3. _____ is the ability of language to refer to contexts removed from the speaker's immediate situation.
4. According to Saussure, _____ refers to the concrete utterances of a speaker.
5. Voicing refers to the _____ of the vocal folds.

II. Determine if each of the following statements is true or false. (5 points/1 point for each)

1. Bound morpheme refers to those which can not occur alone and must appear with at least one other morpheme.
2. "Daybreak" is a compound word, and it belongs to the class of verb compound.
3. The uttering of a performative sentence is, or is a pari of, the doing of an action.
4. During two-word stage, children begin to learn words at a rate of one every two waking hours, and keeps learning that rate or faster through adolescence.
5. Coordination refers to the process or result of linking linguistic units so that they have different syntactic status, one being dependent upon the other, and usually a constituent of the other.

III. Choose the best answer to fill in the following blanks. (5 points/1 point for each)

1. _____ construction is one whose distribution is functionally equivalent to that of one or more of its constituents, i.e., a word or a groups of words, which serves as a definable Center or Head.

   A. Constituent   B. Endocentric   C. Exocentric   D. Connective

2. _____ is made up from the first letters of the name of an organization, which has a heavily modified headword.

   A. Category   B. Synonymy   C. Antonymy   D. Acronym

3. A _____ is what is expressed by a declarative sentence when that sentence is uttered to make a statement.

   A. proposition   B. composition   C. description   D. exposition

4. As an important concept put forward by theoretic linguistics, _____ stands lor the faculty of language in the broad sense.

   A. FLB   B. FLS   C. FLN   D. FLA

5. _____ refers to relations of meaning that exist within the text, and that define it as a text.

   A. Agreement   B. Cohesion   C. Recursiveness   D. Embedding

IV. Fulfill the following requirements. (10 points/5 points for each)

1. Please name some main branches of macrolinguistics. (5 points)
2. Of the following pairs of sentences, please tell whether A entails B in each case. (5 points)

   (1) A. Nancy owns three canaries.
       B. Nancy owns a canary.
   (2) A. John has done his homework.
       B. John hasn't brushed his teeth.

V. Answer each of the following questions briefly. (25 points)

1. Why should language teachers increase their knowledge of linguistics? Please

give some comments. (10 points)
2. What do you think of the contributions that sociolinguistics has made to linguistic studies? (10 points)
3. What's the Critical Period Hypothesis of language acquisition? Please comment on it. (5 points)

Appendixes

Appendix 4
A Comprehensive Exam for MA-TESL Candidates

MA-TESL Comprehensive Exam for January 7, 2014

Instructions for test-takers: This is a "closed book" exam. Thus, you may not use any reference materials while responding; you may not consult notes, books, and/or articles during the examination. If you are writing the examination on the computer, you may not access any additional files or documents that may reside on the computer hard drive or be available through a network, the Internet or any other external website or device, or in your own email.

There are five (5) sections on the test. You must complete **three (3)** of them. All MA-TESL students must take the ESL Foundations and Methods section. MA-TESL students will then **choose two (2)** of the remaining four sections (ESL Curriculum and Program Administration; Second Language Acquisition; Grammar; and Sociolinguistics). PhD students taking the test for screening purposes can answer questions in **any three (3)** sections, but they cannot choose both (a) ESL Foundations and Methods and (b) ESL Curriculum and Program Administration.

You will have **four hours and fifteen minutes** to complete this test. This period includes printing time and any breaks you need to take. You should plan to spend approximately 1 hour and 20 minutes on each section you answer. Each section has two questions, and you must answer both questions. Thus, you should spend approximately 40 minutes per question. Budget your time so that you can quickly review your responses.

Your answers to the questions should be well written, and synthesize relevant knowledge in a coherent and insightful manner. You should include references to specific sources and studies, including current scholarship. We recognize that this test requires rapid written responses, and you should strive to write as clearly and effectively as possible.

- Begin your answer to each question on a new sheet of paper.
- Write the last four (4) digits of your university ID number in the upper right hand corner of each page. (DO NOT write your name on the exam responses.)
- Number your pages.
- Print your responses as you finish each section. Do not wait until you have completed the entire test to begin to print your responses.

Section 1: Foundations and Methods (answer both questions)

1. In discussions of second language acquisition and language teaching, the following terms are often mentioned:

    (1) Interlanguage
    (2) Communicative competence
    (3) Learning styles
    (4) Learning strategies
    (5) Critical period
    (6) Motivation

Select THREE of these terms. For each one, (a) provide a brief definition that reveals its complexity; (b) explain its significance to the language classroom in general; and (c) discuss how these will inform your teaching of English as a second/foreign language. Include concrete examples to illustrate your points. Refer to relevant literature as appropriate. Be sure to include (a) a brief introduction that tells your reader which three terms you plan to discuss and (b) a brief conclusion to provide some closure to your response.

2. Select TWO (and only two) skill areas, from the following list, that can be integrated in classroom instruction: listening, speaking, reading, and writing. Then discuss the two skill areas from the following perspectives:
   a) Briefly identify a teaching situation in which the two skills can be integrated.
   b) Provide a detailed rationale for skill integration in this setting.
   c) Describe the range of teaching techniques and classroom activities that could lead to meaningful skill integration in this setting. Provide an explanation for proposing these specific techniques and activities that demonstrates your understanding of each skill and the needs of L2 learners.

Refer to relevant literature as appropriate. Be sure to include an introduction and conclusion to frame your response.

Section 2: Sociolinguistics (answer both questions)

1. Register comparison/analysis

Read text samples A and B below. Identify 4 or 5 of the most frequent linguistic features found in each one; then compare these two texts, noting two similar linguistic features and two distinctive ones for each. Finally, provide a functional explanation for the similarities and differences observed.

Text A— Excerpt of classroom teaching

Instructor: For today what we need to do is go over your findings for the theories of time and place adverbials. And, talk about if you were gonna write this up, for instance, for a corpus-based mini project, what would it look like, when you write it up? What would you do? And then we'll talk about the lexico grammar chapter. And, then we'll do some lexicogrammatical analysis next class.

[Student raises hand]

Student: OK, the, the, the list that you put on kind of the last overhead from last time, was, I wrote down, association between adverbial and verb.

Instructor: Right.

Student: Um, and-and. that's not the title of what's on the slide. That's one of the items, right?

Instructor: Yep.

Student: OK. Is that, was this, list, um, specifically for, the preferred form that, the place time or was it for all of them that-could-that needs to be examined for each of them.

Instructor: This was a list of ideas of factors you might wanna consider if you were running out of ideas.

Text B—Selection from a linguistics textbook

From an articulatory point of view, consonants and vowels are both made by positioning the vocal tract in a particular configuration. However, consonants are distinguished from vowels in that consonants are produced with a constriction somewhere in the vocal tract that impedes airflow, while vowels have at most only a slight narrowing and allow air to flow freely through the oral cavity. We can also distinguish consonants and vowels acoustically, based on the type of sounds they produce: consonants are much quieter than vowels and usually cannot function as the nucleus of a syllable. The syllable nucleus is the "heart" of the syllable, carrying suprasegmental information such as stress, loudness, and pitch, which vowels are much better suited to do than consonants.

2. Major topics in sociolinguistics

Select three different topics from sociolinguistics that have, in your view, provided information of greatest relevance for applied linguistic research or language teaching in a setting where you have taught or might expect to teach. For each topic, identify at least one empirical study: summarize its research focus and findings, and indicate the implications of this research for further research or for language and literacy instruction in the setting envisioned.

Section 3: Grammar (answer both questious)

1. There are numerous structural devices in English that can be used to vary word order. So, for example, adverbial clauses can be placed at the beginning or end of a main clause. The text passage below, from a classroom lecture, illustrates the use of some of these devices. Describe the grammatical characteristics and discourse functions of <u>three</u> of these structural devices, making reference to the text passage, (*Do not include* the placement of adverbial phrases/clauses as one of your devices.) Be sure to include discussion of the discourse functions that influence the choice between grammatical variants.

And if you do sell stocks, then, usually they should give you the money resulting from the transaction, and this is called "contributed capital" by experts working in the field. The capital is contributed to your company by giving you the money and buying your shares.
[*Long pause*] OK. The presentation is over. Close your eyes, because I'm going to turn the light on. OK?

2. Analyze the following sentences using the diagramming system that you are most familiar with. In your diagrams, label the forms, grammatical functions, and word classes of all words and constituents in each sentence.
a. Usually they should give you the money resulting from the transaction. (Lecture)
b. The capital is contributed to your company by giving you the money. (Lecture)
c. So, how do you think he manages to use that approach? (Lecture)
d. Therefore the company's claim that they improve grades is supported by the evidence. (Lecture)
e. Knowing what I know about law school, you will probably never get the chance to see things from that other side. (Lecture)

Section 4: Curriculum and Program Administration (answer both questions)

1. Imagine that you have applied for a language program position that has a significant administrative component. As part of the application process, you've been asked to explain your approach to resolving administrative issues that you might face as a program administrator. Of the four dilemmas presented below, choose **three** and state: (1) specific steps that could be taken to resolve the dilemma and (2) a rationale for the steps that you propose. Refer to relevant literature to strengthen your answers. The overall response should include a brief introduction and conclusion.

- The program shows signs of stagnation at curricular, staffing, and technological levels.
- The language program is misunderstood by many constituents both on and off campus.
- The majority of language program faculty consider monthly faculty meetings to be a total waste of time. Yet all would agree that meetings are important for the health of the program.
- The language program wants to articulate more closely with other departments on campus to better meet their needs.

2. The course-and curriculum-development process has been described by many in the field. Consider the case of new course development. What are (a) the steps that course designers should take and (b) the decisions that course designers must make to convert a good idea for a new course into a course ready for implementation? Describe the process, starting with early information gathering and continuing through the piloting or implementation phase. Describe **each** step in detail, referring to relevant literature to strengthen your claims. Make sure to include a brief introduction and conclusion to frame your response.

Section 5: Second Language Acquisition (answer both questions)

1. Input & Interaction

Long's interaction hypothesis (1983, 1996) has led to a number of theoretical propositions and a substantial body of research. Address each of the following three issues in your response to this prompt, focusing on **TWO** of the constructs listed below: 1) Identify and describe the constructs you choose. 2) Explain how these two constructs relate to each other and to language learning more generally, both in theory and as described in results found in the empirical literature. And 3) Discuss how the interactionist tradition of SLA has contributed to L2 pedagogy both generally and with respect to the two constructs you've chosen.

negotiation of meaning

negotiation of form

feedback

modified/ comprehensible input

(pushed) output

noticing

2. L2 Vocabulary Development

Much like other areas of SLA (e.g., L2 morphosyntax), lexical development involves the interplay of learner internal, learner external (i.e., environmental), and linguistic variables. In your response to this question, describe (a) the different types of lexical knowledge learners might have, (b) the process by which vocabulary knowledge develops, considering the different types of internal, external, and linguistic variables involved, and (c) the pedagogical implications of research on L2 vocabulary development. Refer to relevant studies as necessary.

责任编辑：陈卫伟

图书在版编目（CIP）数据

语言学习题汇编：英文 / 刘振聪主编. -- 北京：旅游教育出版社，2018.7
 ISBN 978-7-5637-3776-5

Ⅰ. ①语… Ⅱ. ①刘… Ⅲ. ①语言学－英文 Ⅳ. ①H0

中国版本图书馆CIP数据核字(2018)第155568号

语言学习题汇编

刘振聪　主编

贾　彤　耿恺婕　副主编

出版单位	旅游教育出版社
地　　址	北京市朝阳区定福庄南里1号
邮　　编	100024
发行电话	（010）65778403　65728372　65767462（传真）
本社网址	www.tepcb.com
E-mail	tepfx@163.com
排版单位	北京旅教文化传播有限公司
印刷单位	北京虎彩文化传播有限公司
经销单位	新华书店
开　　本	710毫米×1000毫米　1/16
印　　张	16
字　　数	179千字
版　　次	2018年7月第1版
印　　次	2018年7月第1次印刷
定　　价	49.00元

（图书如有装订差错请与发行部联系）